Anglo-Norman England

CONFERENCE ON BRITISH STUDIES
BIBLIOGRAPHICAL HANDBOOKS

Editor: J. JEAN HECHT
Consultant Editor: G. R. ELTON

Anglo-Norman England 1066-1154

MICHAEL ALTSCHUL
CASE WESTERN RESERVE UNIVERSITY

CAMBRIDGE

for the Conference on British Studies

AT THE UNIVERSITY PRESS

1969

Published by the Syndics of the Cambridge University Press
Bentley House, 200 Euston Road, London N.W.1
American Branch: 32 East 57th Street, New York, N.Y. 10022

Standard Book Number: 521 07582 3

Library of Congress Catalogue Card Number 78-80816

Printed in Great Britain by
Alden & Mowbray Ltd
at the Alden Press, Oxford

To My Mother and Father

CONTENTS

Preface   *page* ix

Abbreviations   xi

Explanatory Notes   xi

   I BIBLIOGRAPHIES   1

  II CATALOGUES, GUIDES, AND HANDBOOKS   2

 III GENERAL SURVEYS   6

 IV CONSTITUTIONAL AND ADMINISTRATIVE HISTORY   8

  V POLITICAL HISTORY   18

 VI FOREIGN RELATIONS   25

 VII SOCIAL HISTORY   27

VIII ECONOMIC HISTORY   37

 IX AGRICULTURAL HISTORY   41

  X SCIENCE AND TECHNOLOGY   44

 XI MILITARY AND NAVAL HISTORY   46

 XII RELIGIOUS HISTORY   49

XIII HISTORY OF THE FINE ARTS   62

XIV INTELLECTUAL HISTORY   65

Index of authors, editors, and translators   73

PREFACE

Each period to be covered in this series can lay claim to numerous problems and peculiarities of bibliographical organization; but the arbitrary nature of any scheme of classification is in many ways even more pronounced for the Anglo-Norman period than for more modern ones. Biographies exist only for a few major political and ecclesiastical figures, and most of the latter could be placed in any one of a number of categories with equal validity. I have also included certain biographical articles which seem to me to represent as complete a biography as the sources will permit. 'Foreign Relations' is a misnomer for the eleventh and twelfth centuries, and I have largely confined that section to the major works relating to Scotland, Wales, and France, with the exception of Normandy. There is little in the way of science or technology that can be rooted in the chronological limits of this work. Most importantly, many items, especially those relating to Domesday Book, are simultaneously contributions to varying combinations of administrative, social, economic, agricultural, military, and ecclesiastical history; I have endeavoured to place each where its main emphasis or value seems to lie, but I am convinced that no two scholars would agree for very long as to what should go where. I have deliberately placed as wide an interpretation on 'Religious History' as possible, so that most items relating to the church and its institutional structure, even those sources (mostly cartularies) and secondary works in social and economic history, are to be found in that section. On the other hand, I have placed under 'Intellectual History' works that seemed to me to be of value in reflecting more popular religious and cultural attitudes, as well as those devoted to formal thought. Literature *per se* has been excluded from this compilation, but a few works are included which illuminate more than purely literary questions. It goes without saying that most items in the last section refer to men who happened to be born in England, or who lived there, rather than to 'English' intellectual history; their true frame of reference was not England, but the *respublica christiana*.

In addition to these problems of classification, there are other special problems that call for comment. First, Anglo-Norman England cannot be divorced from Anglo-Saxon England, or Normandy, or even Angevin England. I have therefore included a few of the works basic to these subjects that have a bearing, albeit indirect, on the Anglo-Norman age: works which provide insight into the proper foundations, in time and in space, upon which the structure of Anglo-Norman government and society rested. Secondly, the terminal date 1154 is meaningful only for political and constitutional history, and least meaningful of all for intellectual history and the history of art. For this reason I have included items on such figures as John of Salisbury and others who, while figuring most prominently in the later twelfth century, were also active before this date; by the same token, however, I have not tried to provide exhaustive references to them. Finally, the *VCH* series continues its obsolescent way; I have preferred to give only general references to the volumes in the series (in the 'Surveys' section), with individual references to those items, such as the Domesday introductions by Round, Stenton, and others, that seem of more permanent value and usefulness.

I wish to thank the General Editor of this series, Dr J. Jean Hecht, for his advice and his inexhaustible kindness and patience; Dr Bryce D. Lyon, who generously undertook to read the entire work in typescript; Dr Sidney R. Packard for his help at an early stage; and my wife Marian for her encouragement. The typescript was sent to the publisher in August 1968, and contains no reference to works which have appeared since that date.

MICHAEL ALTSCHUL

Cleveland, Ohio

ABBREVIATIONS

AHR	*American Historical Review*
Arch.	*Archaeologia*
BIHR	*Bulletin of the Institute of Historical Research*
BJRL	*Bulletin of the John Rylands Library*
Camb. Hist. J.	*Cambridge Historical Journal*
CEH	*The Cambridge Economic History of Europe*, ed. Michael M. Postan *et al.*, vols. I (2nd ed.), II–III, Cambridge, 1952–66
CMH	*The Cambridge Medieval History*, ed. John B. Bury *et al.*, Cambridge, 1911–36, 8 vols.
CQR	*Church Quarterly Review*
DGME	*The Domesday Geography of Midland England*, ed. H. Clifford Darby and Ian B. Terrett, Cambridge, 1954
DGNE	*The Domesday Geography of Northern England*, ed. H. Clifford Darby and Ian S. Maxwell, Cambridge, 1962
DGSEE	*The Domesday Geography of South-East England*, ed. H. Clifford Darby and Eila M. J. Campbell, Cambridge, 1962
EcHR	*Economic History Review*
EHR	*English Historical Review*
E.P.-N.S.	English Place-Name Society
FE	J. Horace Round, *Feudal England*, 1895, re-issued 1964
Hist.	*History*
HMSO	Her Majesty's Stationery Office
JBS	*Journal of British Studies*
JEH	*Journal of Ecclesiastical History*
JHI	*Journal of the History of Ideas*
LQR	*Law Quarterly Review*
PP	*Past and Present*
PRO	Public Record Office
RS	Rolls Series
Spec.	*Speculum*
Trad.	*Traditio*
TRHS	*Transactions of the Royal Historical Society*
VCH	*The Victoria History of the Counties of England*
Yorks. Arch. J.	*Yorkshire Archaeological Journal*

EXPLANATORY NOTES

1. Unless otherwise specified, London is the place of publication.

2. Cross-references fall into two major groups, substantive and bibliographical. A substantive cross-reference is indicated by the author's name and the item number, as follows: 'see also Milne (23)', except that in the case of another work by the same author, his name is not repeated. Bibliographical references are to the

initial (full) citation of collected or collective works; if the entry contains critical comment, the cross-reference is placed immediately after the shortened title in brackets, as follows: '*Studies . . . Powicke* [see (390)], pp. 76–89'. Where there are no critical comments, the cross-reference is placed at the very end of the entry, as follows: '*Studies . . . Powicke*, pp. 1–14. See (390)'.

I BIBLIOGRAPHIES

1 Bellot, H. Hale and A. Taylor Milne. *Writings on British history 1901–1933* (Royal Historical Society). 1968–, 5 vols. in 7 pts. Vols. I–II, *Auxiliary sciences and general works*, and *The middle ages, 450–1485* (1968), are relevant for the Anglo-Norman period. See also Milne (23).
2 Besterman, Theodore. *A world bibliography of bibliographies*. 4th ed., Lausanne, 1965–6, 5 vols.
3 Bonser, Wilfrid. *An Anglo-Saxon and Celtic bibliography (450–1087)*. 1957. Comprehensive bibliography to 1953.
4 *Bulletin bibliographique de la Société Internationale Arthurienne*. Paris, 1949–. Useful for Arthurian material illustrative of problems wider than purely literary.
5 Cam, Helen M. and Arthur S. Turberville. *Bibliography of English constitutional history* (Historical Association Leaflets, no. 25). 1929. Short but useful.
6 Caron, Pierre and Marc Jaryc (eds.). *World list of historical periodicals and bibliographies*. Oxford, 1939.
7 Chevallier, Ulysse. *Répertoire des sources historiques du moyen âge: bio-bibliographique*. Paris, 1905–7, 2 vols.
8 —— *Répertoire des sources historiques du moyen âge: topo-bibliographique*. Paris, 1894–1903, 2 vols.
9 Chrimes, Stanley B. and Ivan Alan Roots. *English constitutional history: a select bibliography* (Historical Association, Helps for Students of History, no. 58). 1958. More recent and fuller than Cam (5).
10 Courtauld Institute of Art. *Annual bibliography of the history of British art, 1934–*. 1936–.
11 Français, Jean. *Bibliotheque générale des ecrivains de l'Ordre de Saint-Benoît*. Bouillon, 1777–8, 4 vols. Biographies and works of Benedictines. Largely superseded by Kapsner (19).
12 Frère, Edouard. *Manuel du bibliographie normand*. Rouen, 1858–60, 2 vols. Still a valuable guide.
13 Gross, Charles. *The sources and literature of English history*. 2nd ed., 1915. Goes to 1910. Still the only comprehensive medieval bibliography, but obsolete by now. A new ed. is in preparation.
14 —— *Bibliography of municipal history*. Cambridge, Mass., 1897. This, Hall (15) and Moore (24) are still useful, but the best starting-points for economic and agrarian history are the bibliographies for Postan (1040 and 1130).
15 Hall, Hubert. *Select bibliography for the study, sources, and literature of English medieval economic history*. 1914.
16 Hoyt, Robert S. and Peter H. Sawyer (eds.). *International medieval bibliography*. Minneapolis and Leeds, 1967–. A new and highly important project, designed to provide an exhaustive bibliography of article literature on all phases of medieval history, from 1967. Bibliographies are issued quarterly in card form, and a book form is also planned.
17 Humphreys, Arthur L. *A handbook to county bibliography*. 1917. Useful for local history.
18 Jenkins, Rhys T. and William Rees (eds.). *Bibliography of the history of Wales*. 2nd ed., Cardiff, 1962. The basic guide to Welsh history, and very useful for Norman–Welsh relations.
19 Kapsner, Oliver L. *A Benedictine bibliography*. 2nd ed., Collegeville, Minn., 1962, 2 vols. Supersedes Français (11).
20 Lyon, Bryce D. 'From Hengist and Horsa to Edward of Caernarvon: recent writings on English history', in Elizabeth Chapin Furber (ed.), *Changing views on British history*. Cambridge, Mass., 1966, pp. 1–57. Survey of scholarship, 1939–62.
21 Marquet de Vasselot, Alphonse J. J. *Bibliographie de la tapisserie, des tapis*

et de la broderie en France. Paris, 1935. Includes a bibliography on the
Bayeux tapestry.

22 Maxwell, William H. *A bibliography of English law to 1650.* 1925.
23 Milne, A. Taylor. *Writings on British history, 1934–1945* (Royal Historical
Society). 1937–60, 8 vols. Comprehensive annual bibliographies, arranged
chronologically and topically. See also Bellot and Milne (1).
24 Moore, Margaret A. *A classified list of works relating to English manorial
and agrarian history, from the earliest times to the year 1660* (London
School of Economics, Studies in Economics, Bibliographies, no. 2).
1912.
25 Paetow, Louis J. *Guide to the study of medieval history,* ed. Dana C. Munro
and Gray C. Boyce. New York, 1931. Still useful, but quite obsolescent.
A new ed. is planned.
26 Potthast, August. *Bibliotheca historica medii aevi.* 2nd ed., Berlin, 1896, 2 vols.
A new ed. of this great work, entitled *Repertorium fontium historiae medii
aevi,* is in progress; 2 vols. have appeared to date (1962, 1967).
27 *Répertoire bibliographique de l'histoire de France.* Paris, 1923–38, 15 vols.
Detailed bibliography of works on French history from 1920 to 1931.
The series was resumed for works published since 1955 as *Bibliographie
annuelle de l'histoire de France,* Paris, 1956–. A supplementary series to
cover the period 1931–1954 is in progress; 1 vol., *Années 1953–1954,* has
appeared to date (1964).
28 Stein, Henri. *Bibliographie générale des cartulaires français.* Paris, 1907.
29 —— *Manuel de bibliographie générale.* Paris, 1898.
30 US Department of Health. *Bibliography of the history of medicine.* Washington, D.C., 1965–. Issued annually.
31 Upcott, William. *Bibliographical account of the principal works relating to
English topography.* 1818, 3 vols. Useful guide to the great antiquarian
histories compiled in the seventeenth and eighteenth centuries.
32 Whitney, James P. *Bibliography of church history* (Historical Association
Leaflets, no. 55). 1923.

II CATALOGUES, GUIDES, AND HANDBOOKS

33 Atkinson, Thomas D. *Glossary of terms used in English architecture.* 7th ed.,
1948.
34 Bannister, Arthur T. *Descriptive catalogue of the manuscripts in the Hereford
Cathedral Library.* Hereford, 1927.
35 Baugh, Albert C. *History of the English language.* 1935.
36 Baxter, James H. and Charles Johnson. *Medieval Latin word-list from British
and Irish sources.* 1934. A basic dictionary, but now superseded by Latham
(98).
37 Birch, Walter de Gray. *Catalogue of seals in the department of manuscripts in
the British Museum.* 1887–1900, 6 vols.
38 Bishop, Terence A. *Scriptores regis.* Oxford, 1961. Plates to identify hands
of twelfth-century scribes.
39 Boutell, Charles. *Boutell's heraldry,* ed. Charles W. Scott-Giles and John P.
Brooke-Little. 1963.
40 Brendon, John A. *Dictionary of English history.* 1937.
41 Britton, Charles E. *A meteorological chronology to A.D. 1450.* 1937.
42 Cabrol, Fernand and Henri Leclerq (eds.). *Dictionnaire d'archéologie
chrétienne et de liturgie.* Paris, 1903–53, 15 vols.
43 Cheney, Christopher R. *Handbook of dates for students of English history*
(Royal Historical Society guides and handbooks, no. 4). 2nd ed., 1961.
An indispensable reference work.
44 Christopher, Henry G. T. *Palaeography and archives.* 1938.

45 Cokayne, George E. *The complete peerage of England, Scotland, Ireland, Great Britain and the United Kingdom* . . . , ed. Vicary Gibbs *et al.* 1910–49, 13 vols. The great authoritative guide, but complicated and awkward to use. For most matters of Norman genealogy, it is advisable to start with Sanders (122).

46 Cottineau, Lawrence H. *Répertoire topo-bibliographique des abbayes et prieurés.* Mâcon, 1935, 2 vols.

47 Cross, Frank L. (ed.). *Oxford dictionary of the Christian church.* Oxford, 1957.

48 Davis, Godfrey R. C. *Medieval cartularies of Great Britain: a short catalogue.* 1958. Valuable guide to printed and unprinted cartularies.

49 Denholm-Young, Noel. *Handwriting in England and Wales.* Cardiff, 1954. Generally useful, but erratic in supplying transcripts.

50 de Ricci, Seymour. *Census of medieval and Renaissance manuscripts in the United States and Canada.* New York, 1935–40, 3 vols.

51 Du Cange, Charles. *Glossarium mediae et infimae latinitatis.* New ed., Paris, 1883–7, 5 vols. in 10 pts. The great dictionary, but less useful for English history than Latham (98).

52 Ekwall, B. O. Eilert. *Concise Oxford dictionary of English place-names.* 4th ed., Oxford, 1960.

53 Floyer, John K. and Sidney G. Hamilton. *Catalogue of manuscripts preserved in the chapter library of Worcester Cathedral* (Worcestershire Historical Society, xx). Worcester, 1920.

54 Fowler, G. Herbert. 'Notes on the pronunciation of medieval Latin in England', *Hist.*, new ser., **22** (Sept. 1937), 97–109.

55 Galbraith, Vivian H. 'Handwriting', in Austin Lane Poole (ed.), *Medieval England.* Oxford, 1958, 2 vols., II, 541–58.

56 —— *Introduction to the use of the public records.* Oxford, 1934. Indispensable.

57 Giry, Arthur. *Manuel de diplomatique.* Paris, 1894. A standard work.

58 Giuseppi, Montague S. *Guide to the manuscripts preserved in the Public Record Office.* 1923–4, 2 vols. Now superseded by the new HMSO *Guide* (61).

59 Grant, Francis J. *Manual of heraldry.* Revised ed., Edinburgh, 1929.

60 HMSO. *Ancient monuments and historical buildings* (Sectional List, no. 27). Issued annually; guide to the publications of the Royal Commission on the Ancient and Historical Monuments and Constructions of England.

61 —— *Guide to the contents of the Public Record Office.* 1963, 2 vols. Supersedes Giuseppi (58); current to 1960.

62 —— *Publications of the Royal Commission on Historical Manuscripts* (Sectional List, no. 17). Issued annually.

63 —— *Record publications* (Sectional List, no. 24). Issued annually; guide to the publications of the PRO, the Record Commission, the Rolls Series, *et al.*

64 Hall, Hubert. *Formula book of English official historical documents.* Cambridge, 1908–9, 2 pts. Documents representing various classes of diplomatic and legal records.

65 —— *Repertory of British archives, Part I: England.* 1920.

66 Hardy, Thomas Duffus. *Descriptive catalogue of materials relating to the history of Great Britain and Ireland* (RS, no. 26). 1862–71, 3 vols. Still an essential work; vol. II covers the period 1066–1200.

67 Harvey, Henry P. *The Oxford companion to English literature.* 2nd ed., Oxford, 1937.

68 Hector, Leonard C. *The handwriting of English documents.* 2nd ed., 1966. The best general introduction to English paleography and diplomatics.

69 James, Montague Rhodes. *The ancient libraries of Canterbury and Dover.* Cambridge, 1903.

70 —— *Descriptive catalogue of the Latin manuscripts in the John Rylands Library at Manchester.* Manchester, 1921, 2 vols. Supplemented by annual notices of recent accessions and acquisitions, printed in the *BJRL*.

71 —— *Descriptive catalogue of the manuscripts in the college library of Magdalene College, Cambridge.* Cambridge, 1909.

3

72 —— *Descriptive catalogue of the manuscripts in the FitzWilliam Museum.* Cambridge, 1895.

73 —— *Descriptive catalogue of the manuscripts in the library of Corpus Christi College, Cambridge.* Cambridge, 1909–12, 2 vols.

74 —— *Descriptive catalogue of the manuscripts in the library of Eton College.* Cambridge, 1895.

75 —— *Descriptive catalogue of the manuscripts in the library of Gonville and Caius College.* Cambridge, 1907–14, 2 vols.

76 —— *Descriptive catalogue of the manuscripts in the library of Jesus College, Cambridge.* Cambridge, 1895.

77 —— *Descriptive catalogue of the manuscripts . . . in the library of King's College, Cambridge.* Cambridge, 1895.

78 —— *Descriptive catalogue of the manuscripts in the library of Pembroke College, Cambridge.* Cambridge, 1905.

79 —— *Descriptive catalogue of the manuscripts in the library of Peterhouse . . .* Cambridge, 1899.

80 —— *Descriptive catalogue of the manuscripts in the library of St. John's College, Cambridge.* Cambridge, 1913.

81 —— *Descriptive catalogue of the manuscripts in the library of Sidney Sussex College, Cambridge.* Cambridge, 1895.

82 —— *Descriptive catalogue of the western manuscripts in the library of Christ's College, Cambridge.* Cambridge, 1905.

83 —— *Descriptive catalogue of the western manuscripts in the library of Clare College, Cambridge.* Cambridge, 1905.

84 —— *Descriptive catalogue of the western manuscripts in the library of Queen's College, Cambridge.* Cambridge, 1905.

85 —— *The manuscripts in the library at Lambeth Palace* (Cambridge Antiquarian Society Publications, Octavo Series, no. 33). Cambridge, 1900.

86 —— *The western manuscripts in the library of Emmanuel College. A descriptive catalogue.* Cambridge, 1904.

87 —— *The western manuscripts in the library of Trinity College, Cambridge. A descriptive catalogue.* Cambridge, 1900–4, 4 vols.

88 Jesperson, J. Otto. *The growth and structure of the English language.* 9th ed., Leipzig, 1938.

89 Johnson, Charles and Hilary Jenkinson. *English court hand 1066–1500.* Oxford, 1915, 2 vols. The basic guide to paleography and diplomatics; vol. II has numerous plates from the Anglo-Norman period.

90 Jones, Philip and Raymond Smith. *Guide to the records in the Corporation of London Records Office and the Guildhall Library muniment room.* 1951.

91 Ker, Neil R. *Catalogue of manuscripts containing Anglo-Saxon.* Oxford, 1957.

92 —— *English manuscripts in the century after the Norman Conquest.* Oxford, 1960. With numerous plates; excellent for paleographical work.

93 —— *Medieval libraries of Great Britain: a list of surviving books* (Royal Historical Society guides and handbooks, no. 3). 2nd ed., 1964.

94 —— *Medieval manuscripts in British libraries.* Oxford, forthcoming. Vol. I, *London,* has been announced.

95 Knowles, David and Richard N. Hadcock, *Medieval religious houses: England and Wales.* 1953. Indispensable. See also *idem,* 'Additions and corrections', *EHR,* 72 (Jan. 1957), 60–87.

96 Kunitz, Stanley J. and Howard Haycraft. *British authors before 1800: a biographical dictionary.* New York, 1952.

97 Kurath, Hans, Sherman Kuhn and John Reidy (eds.). *Middle English dictionary.* Ann Arbor, 1954–.

98 Latham, Ronald E. *Revised medieval Latin word-list from British and Irish sources.* 1965. Supersedes Baxter and Johnson (36).

99 London University, Institute of Historical Research. 'Historical manuscripts: accessions; migrations'. Published annually in the *BIHR.*

100 Low, Sidney and Frederic S. Pulling, *Dictionary of English history.* Revised ed., 1928.

101 Macray, William Dunn. *Manual of British historians to A.D. 1600.* 1845.

102 Madan, Falconer *et al. Summary catalogue of western manuscripts in the Bodleian Library*. Oxford, 1895–1953, 7 vols.
103 Martin, Charles Trice. *The record interpreter*. 2nd ed., 1910. Invaluable guide to abbreviations; also contains a useful glossary.
104 Meyer, Otto and Renate Klauser. *Clavis Mediaevalis: Kleines Wörterbuch der Mittelalterforschung*. Wiesbaden, 1962. An excellent glossary of terms employed in fields usually classified as 'ancillary' to history, e.g. heraldry, numismatics.
105 Millar, Eric G. (ed.). *A descriptive catalogue of the western manuscripts in the library of A. Chester Beatty*. 1927, 4 vols.
106 Mitchell, Jean (ed.). *Great Britain: geographical essays*. Cambridge, 1962. Useful for topographical background.
107 Mullins, Edward L. C. *Texts and calendars: an analytical guide to serial publications* (Royal Historical Society guides and handbooks, no. 7). 1958. An indispensable annotated guide to the publications of government bodies (e.g. Record Commission, RS, PRO), 'national' societies (e.g. Pipe Roll Society), and local (county) record societies. Complete to 1957.
108 Mynors, Roger A. B. (ed.). *Catalogue of the manuscripts of Balliol College, Oxford*. Oxford, 1963.
109 —— (ed.). *Durham Cathedral manuscripts to the end of the twelfth century*. Oxford, 1939. Includes numerous facsimiles.
110 New Palaeographical Society. *Facsimiles of ancient manuscripts*. 1903–12, 2 vols. (1st ser.); 1913–32, 2 vols. (2nd ser.).
111 Niermeyer, Jan F. *Mediae Latinitatis lexicon minus*. Leiden, 1954–. In progress. Latin–French–English dictionary, from the mid-sixth to the mid-twelfth centuries.
112 Palaeographical Society. *Facsimiles of ancient manuscripts*. 1873–83, 3 vols. (1st ser.); 1884–94, 2 vols. (2nd ser.).
113 Parker, James. *A glossary of terms used in heraldry*, 2nd ed., Oxford, 1894.
114 Peck, Heather and Catherine Hall (eds.). *The archives of the university of Cambridge*. Cambridge, 1962.
115 Poole, Reginald Lane. 'The beginning of the year in the middle ages', in *Studies in chronology and history*, ed. Austin Lane Poole, Oxford, 1934, pp. 1–27.
116 —— (ed.). *Historical atlas of modern Europe*. Oxford 1896–1900, 2 vols. Includes an excellent map of England in 1806 by James Tait.
117 —— 'Seals and documents', in Poole, *Studies in chronology and history* [see (115)], pp. 90–111. A very useful general introduction.
118 Powicke, F. Maurice and Edmund B. Fryde. *Handbook of British chronology* (Royal Historical Society guides and handbooks, no. 2). 2nd ed., 1961. An invaluable guide for a wide range of matters, including lists of the chief officers of state, lists of titled nobility, archiepiscopal and episcopal succession, etc.
119 Reaney, Percy H. *Dictionary of British surnames*. 1958.
120 Rees, William. *An historical atlas of Wales*. New ed., 1959.
121 Salter, Herbert E. *Facsimiles of early charters in Oxford muniment rooms*. Oxford, 1929. Excellent vehicle for paleographical work.
122 Sanders, Ivor John. *English baronies. A study of their origin and descent 1086–1327*. Oxford, 1960. Very serviceable for introductory genealogical information.
123 Sawyer, Peter H. *Anglo-Saxon charters: an annotated list and bibliography* (Royal Historical Society guides and handbooks, no. 8). 1968. Excellent guide to the various printed eds. of extant Anglo-Saxon charters.
124 Seligman, Erwin R. (ed.). *Encyclopedia of the social sciences*. 1930–5, 15 vols.
125 Steinberg, Sigfrid H. *Historical tables*. 8th ed., 1966. Useful for comparative chronology.
126 —— *A new dictionary of British history*. 1964.
127 Stephen, Leslie and Sidney Lee (eds.). *Dictionary of national biography*. 1885–1903, 63 vols. Still basic, although usually at least obsolescent in treatment of individuals.

128 Stratmann, Franz H. *Dictionary of the Old English anguage*. 3rd ed., Krefeld, 1878–81, 2 vols.
129 —— *Middle English dictionary*. New ed., Oxford, 1891.
130 Stratton, Arthur. *Introductory handbook to the styles of English architecture*. 3rd ed., 1938, 2 vols.
131 Thomson, Samuel K. 'The criteria of Latin palaeography in the study of Norman documents', *Romanic Review*, **29** (Apr. 1938), 112–19.
132 Vacant, J. M. Alfred *et al*. *Dictionnaire de théologie catholique*. Paris, 1899–1950, 15 vols.
133 Van Caenegem, Raoul C. and François Ganshof. *Kurze Quellenkunde des europäischen Mittelalters*. Göttingen, 1964. A most valuable guide to the major published and unpublished source collections.
134 Warner, George F. and Henry J. Ellis. *Facsimiles of royal and other charters in the British Museum*. Vol. I, *William I–Richard I*. 1903.
135 Wells, John E. *A manual of the writings in Middle English, 1050–1400*. New Haven, 1916. With *Supplements* by Wells *et al*., New Haven, 1919–.
136 Willard, James F. and S. Harrison Thomson, *Progress of medieval and renaissance studies in the United States and Canada*. Boulder, 1923–.
137 Williams, Harry F. *An index of medieval studies published in Festschriften, 1865–1946*. Berkeley. 1951.
138 Winfield, Percy H. *The chief sources of English legal history*. Cambridge, Mass., 1925.
139 Wright, Andrew. *Court hand restored*, ed. Charles Trice Martin. 1879. Old but still serviceable for paleography and diplomatics.
140 Wright, Cyril E. *English vernacular hands*. Oxford, 1960. Useful plates for Old English and Middle English hands.

III GENERAL SURVEYS

141 Adkins, W. Ryland *et al*. *VCH Northampton*. 1902–37, 4 vols.
142 Baker, Timothy. *The Normans*. 1966.
143 Barlow, Frank. *The feudal kingdom of England 1042–1216*. 2nd ed., 1962. The best brief survey.
144 Barrow, Geoffrey W. S. *Feudal Britain*. 1956. Covers the period 1066–1314, with more attention to Wales, Scotland and Ireland than is usual in such books.
145 Bateson, Edward *et al*. *A history of Northumberland*. Newcastle-upon-Tyne, 1893–1940, 15 vols. A companion and completion of Hodgson (782).
146 Bateson, Mary. *Medieval England, 1066–1350*. 1905.
147 Bloch, Marc. *La société féodale*. Paris, 1939–40, 2 vols. Engl. trans. 1960.
148 Boutruche, Robert. *Seigneurie et féodalité*, vol. I. Paris, 1959. Similar to, and in respects superior to, Bloch (147).
149 Brooke, Christopher N. L. *Europe in the central middle ages, 962–1154*. 1964. A recent and imaginative text.
150 —— *From Alfred to Henry III, 871–1272*. Edinburgh, 1961. A lively textbook.
151 Brooke, Zachary N. *History of Europe, 911–1199*. 3rd ed., 1951.
152 Bryant, Arthur. *The medieval foundations of England*. New York, 1967. Popularization.
153 Calmette, Joseph L. *Le monde féodal*. 3rd ed., Paris, 1942.
154 Cam, Helen M. *England before Elizabeth*, 1950. A uniformly good popular introduction.
155 Cantor, Norman. *The English*. New York, 1967.
156 Doubleday, H. Arthur *et al*. *VCH Hampshire*. 1900–12, 5 vols.
157 Douglas, David C. and George W. Greenaway. *English historical documents*, vol. II, *1042–1189*. 1953. A massive and superbly chosen collection of

sources in translation, with excellent topical bibliographies. It is placed here because it is unclassifiable under only one topical rubric—it illuminates every phase of Anglo-Norman history.

158 Farrer, William *et al. VCH Lancaster.* 1906–14, 8 vols.
159 Ganshof, François. *Feudalism,* trans. Philip Grierson. 2nd Engl. ed., New York, 1961. Not a synthesis in the sense of Bloch (147) or Boutruche (148), but very valuable as a survey of comparative institutions.
160 Heer, Friedrich. *Aufgang Europas.* Vienna, 1949. An imaginative, but often forced, interpretative essay, contrasting the 'open' nature of twelfth-century French society and thought with England and Germany, seen as more retrograde (Germany especially so).
161 Hollister, C. Warren. *The making of England, 55 B.C.–1399.* Boston, 1966. A clear, well-written popular account.
162 London County Council (= Greater London Council). *Survey of London.* 1900–. In progress; 34 vols. to date. A detailed topography.
163 Lopez, Robert. *The birth of Europe.* Trans., New York, 1967. A stimulating interpretative textbook, of great value for its larger view of European history and for its superb illustrations.
164 Loyn, Henry R. *The Norman Conquest.* 1965. Probably the best of the more recent accounts, short but stimulating, and paying equal attention to all aspects of society.
165 Malden, Henry E. *et al. VCH Surrey.* 1902–12, 4 vols.
166 Matthew, Donald J. A. *The Norman Conquest.* 1966. A good introduction, similar to Loyn (164).
167 Page, William *et al. VCH Bedford.* 1904–12, 3 vols.
168 —— *VCH Berkshire.* 1906–24, 4 vols.
169 —— *VCH Buckingham.* 1905–27, 4 vols.
170 —— *VCH Cornwall.* 1906–. Vol. I only so far published, although the Domes-day section was published separately as 'Part 8', 1924.
171 —— *VCH Derby.* 1905–. Vols. I–II only so far published.
172 —— *VCH Devon.* 1906–. Vol. I only so far published.
173 —— *VCH Dorset.* 1908–. Vol. II only so far published.
174 —— *VCH Durham.* 1905–28, 3 vols.
175 —— *VCH Essex.* 1903–66, 5 vols. Supplementary bibliographical vol. also published, 1959.
176 —— *VCH Gloucester.* 1907–. Vols. II and VI only so far published.
177 —— *VCH Hereford.* 1908–. Vol. I only so far published.
178 —— *VCH Hertford.* 1902–14, 4 vols.
179 —— *VCH Huntingdon.* 1922–36, 3 vols.
180 —— *VCH Kent.* 1908–. Vols. I–III only so far published.
181 —— *VCH Leicester.* 1907–64, 5 vols.
182 —— *VCH Lincoln.* 1906–. Vol. II only so far published.
183 —— *VCH London.* 1909–. Vol. I only so far published.
184 —— *VCH Middlesex.* 1911–. Vols. II–III only so far published.
185 —— *VCH Norfolk.* 1906–. Vols. I–II only so far published.
186 —— *VCH Nottingham.* 1906–. Vols. I–II only so far published.
187 —— *VCH Oxford.* 1907–. Vols. I–II, V–VIII only so far published.
188 —— *VCH Rutland.* 1908–35, 2 vols.
189 —— *VCH Shropshire.* 1908–. Vol. I only so far published.
190 —— *VCH Somerset.* 1906–. Vols. I–II only so far published.
191 —— *VCH Stafford.* 1908–. Vols. I, IV–V, VIII only so far published.
192 —— *VCH Suffolk.* 1907–. Vols. I–II only so far published.
193 —— *VCH Sussex.* 1905–. Vols. I–IV, VII, IX only so far published.
194 —— *VCH Warwick.* 1904–64, 7 vols.
195 —— *VCH York.* 1912–. Vols. II–IV only so far published.
196 —— *VCH York North Riding.* 1914–23, 2 vols.
197 Palgrave, Francis. *The rise and progress of the English commonwealth.* 1832, 2 pts.
198 Poole, Austin Lane. *From Domesday Book to Magna Carta.* 2nd ed., Oxford, 1955. The 3rd vol. of the Oxford History of England series, and the best of the more detailed surveys.

199 Pugh, Ralph B. *et al. VCH Wiltshire.* 1952–65, 8 vols.
200 Salzman, Louis F. *et al. VCH Cambridge and the Isle of Ely.* 1937–59, 4 vols.
201 Sayles, George O. *Medieval foundations of England.* 2nd ed., 1950. Very full account from Roman times to 1272, with a concluding chapter expressing most clearly and forcibly the Richardson–Sayles interpretation of the origins and nature of parliament.
202 Southern, Richard W. *The making of the middle ages.* New Haven, 1953. Suggestive rather than exhaustive account of eleventh- to twelfth-century society, particularly strong on religious and intellectual matters.
203 Stenton, Doris M. *English society in the early middle ages (1066–1307).* 2nd ed., Harmondsworth, 1952. One of the better vols. in the Pelican History of England series.
204 Stenton, Frank M. *Anglo-Saxon England.* 2nd ed., Oxford, 1947. Standard account of the Anglo-Saxon period, with a thorough-going final section on the Norman achievement. The 2nd vol. of the Oxford History of England series.
205 Whitelock, Dorothy. 'The Anglo-Saxon achievement', in C. T. Chevallier (ed.), *The Norman Conquest,* 1966, pp. 15–43. Included here as the best starting-point for a knowledge of the Anglo-Saxon period as necessary background for Anglo-Norman England.
206 Willis-Bund, John W. *et al. VCH Worcester.* 1901–24, 4 vols.
207 Wilson, James *et al. VCH Cumberland.* 1901–. Vols. I–II only so far published.

IV CONSTITUTIONAL AND ADMINISTRATIVE HISTORY

1 Printed Sources

208 Attenborough, Frederick L. (ed.). *Laws of the earliest English kings.* Cambridge, 1922.
209 Bémont, Charles (ed.). *Chartes des libertés anglaises, 1100–1305.* Paris, 1892.
210 Bigelow, Melville M. (ed.). *Placita Anglo-Normannica.* 1879.
211 Birch, Walter de Gray (ed.). *Cartularium Saxonicum.* 1885–99, 4 vols.
212 —— *Historical charters and constitutional documents of the city of London.* 1887.
213 Bishop, Terence A. and Pierre Chaplais (eds.). *Facsimiles of English royal writs to A.D. 1100 presented to Vivian Hunter Galbraith.* Oxford, 1957.
214 Cronne, Henry A. and Ralph H. C. Davis (eds.). *Regesta Stephani 1135–1154 (Regesta regum Anglo-Normannorum 1066–1154,* vol. III). Oxford, 1967.
215 D'Anisy, Louis Léchaudé (ed.). *Grands rôles des échiquiers de Normandie* (Mémoires de la Société des Antiquaires de Normandie). Paris, 1845.
216 Davies, J. Conway (ed.). *The cartae antiquae (rolls 11–20)* (Pipe Roll Society, LXXI, new ser., XXXIII). 1957.
217 Davis, Henry W. C. (ed.). *Regesta Willelmi Conquestoris et Willelmi Rufi 1066–1100 (Regesta regum Anglo-Normannorum 1066–1154,* vol. I). Oxford, 1913.
218 Dugdale, William. *Origines juridiciales.* 2nd ed., 1671.
219 Fauroux, Marie (ed.). *Recueil des actes des ducs de Normandie de 911 à 1066* (Société des Antiquaires de Normandie). Caen, 1961.
220 HMSO. *Calendar of charter rolls, 1226–1516.* 1903–27, 6 vols. Includes exemplifications of many Anglo-Norman charters.
221 —— *Calendar of documents preserved in France, 918–1206,* ed. J. Horace Round. 1899. Listed as 'Vol. I', but no more published.
222 —— *List of sheriffs for England and Wales from the earliest times to 1831* (PRO Lists and Indexes, no. 9). 1898.

223 —— *Syllabus, in English, of the documents relating to England and other kingdoms contained in . . . Rymer's Foedera,* ed. Thomas Duffus Hardy. 1869–85, 3 vols. For Rymer, see (239). Vol. I of the *Syllabus* covers the period 1066–1377.

224 Hall, Hubert (ed.). *Red Book of the exchequer* (RS, no. 99). 1896, 3 vols. Vol. I contains scutages and charters; vol. III the text of the 'Constitutio domus regis', superseded in Johnson (229).

225 Harmer, Florence E. (ed.). *Anglo-Saxon writs.* Manchester, 1952.

226 Haskins, Charles Homer (ed.). 'The Norman "Consuetudines et Iusticie" of William the Conqueror', *EHR,* **23** (July 1908), 502–8.

227 Hearne, Thomas (ed.). *Liber niger scaccarii.* 2nd ed., 1774, 2 vols.

228 Henderson, William G. (ed.). *Liber pontificalis Christophori Bainbridge archiepiscopi Eboracensis* (Surtees Society, LXI). Durham, 1875. Includes the text of the *Laudes* employed at the coronation of Queen Matilda (1068).

229 Johnson, Charles (ed.). *Dialogus de scaccario.* 1950. The best text and translation.

230 Johnson, Charles and Henry A. Cronne (eds.). *Regesta Henrici Primi 1100–1135 (Regesta regum Anglo-Normannorum,* vol. II). Oxford, 1956.

231 Landon, Lionel (ed.). *The cartae antiquae, rolls 1–10* (Pipe Roll Society, LV, new ser., XVII). 1938. Various charters, from William I to Henry III.

232 Legg, J. Wickham (ed.). *Three coronation orders* (Henry Bradshaw Society. XIX). 1900. Includes an *ordo* composed *c.* 1077–85.

233 Legg, L. G. Wickham (ed.). *English coronation records.* 1901.

234 Liebermann, Felix (ed.). *Die Gesetze der Angel-Sachsen.* Halle, 1903–16, 3 vols.

235 —— *Quadripartitus.* Halle, 1896. Text of the law-book *c.* 1114.

236 Madox, Thomas (ed.). *Formulare Anglicanum.* 1702.

237 Pellens, Karl (ed.). *Die Texte des normannischen Anonymus.* Wiesbaden, 1966. Supersedes the text published in Monumenta Germaniae Historica, *Libelli de Lite,* vol. III, Hannover, 1897.

238 Record Commission. *Ancient laws and institutes of England. . .,* ed. Benjamin Thorpe. 1840, 2 vols.

239 —— *Foedera, conventiones, litterae, et cujuscunque generis acta publica . . . ,* ed. Thomas Rymer, revised by Adam Clarke *et al.* 1816–69, 4 vols. The Record Commission ed. covers only the period 1066–1383; the complete Rymer was first published 1727–35, 20 vols., new ed., The Hague, 1737–45, 10 vols.

240 —— *Magnus rotulus scaccarii, vel magnus rotulus pipae, anno tricesimo-primo regni Henrici Primi . . . ,* ed. Joseph Hunter. 1833. The text of the sole extant pipe roll of the Anglo-Norman period. There is an HMSO reissue of the text, with corrections by Charles Johnson, 1929.

241 —— *Statutes of the realm,* ed. Anthony Luders *et al.* 1810–28, 11 vols. The early texts are largely superseded by Bémont (209).

242 Robertson, Agnes Jane (ed.). *Anglo-Saxon charters.* 2nd ed., Cambridge, 1956. Includes the 1084 Northamptonshire Geld Roll.

243 —— *The laws of the kings of England from Edmund to Henry I.* Cambridge, 1925.

244 Stapleton, Thomas (ed.). *Magni rotuli scaccarii Normanniae sub regibus Angliae.* 1840–4, 2 vols.

245 Stevenson, William H. (ed.). 'A contemporary description of the Domesday survey', *EHR,* **22** (Jan. 1907), 72–84.

246 Stubbs, William. *Select charters . . . ,* 9th ed. by Henry W. C. Davis, Oxford, 1921. The standard collection of texts.

247 Van Caenegem, Raoul C. (ed.). *Royal writs in England from the Conquest to Glanvill* (Selden Society, LXXVII). 1959. Besides printing many documents, this work contains an exhaustive monographic study of writ jurisdiction, arguing for a gradual evolution from Anglo-Saxon times; for the fullest statement of the opposite interpretation, see Doris M. Stenton (268).

2 Surveys

248 Adams, George B. *Constitutional history of England*, ed. Robert S. Schuyler. New York, 1934. Largely a specimen of old-fashioned insular congratulation.

249 —— *Origin of the English constitution.* 2nd ed., New Haven, 1920. Basically a collection, with some re-working, of specialized article literature.

250 Chrimes, Stanley B. *English constitutional history.* 3rd ed., Oxford, 1967. A brief and reliable introduction.

251 —— *Introduction to the administrative history of medieval England.* 3rd ed., Oxford, 1966. An excellent synthesis of specialized work.

252 Gneist, Heinrich Rudolph von. *History of the English constitution.* 1891, 2 vols.

253 Harding, Alan. *Social history of English law.* Harmondsworth, 1966.

254 Haskins, George L. *Growth of English representative government.* Philadelphia, 1948. Best short introduction to the growth of parliament, but too ready to posit a rosy tradition of mutual 'counsel and consent' between king and baronage as a root.

255 Holdsworth, William S. *History of English law.* 7th ed., by Stanley B. Chrimes *et al.* 1956–66, 16 vols.

256 Jolliffe, John E. A. *Constitutional history of medieval England.* 4th ed., 1962. An imaginative but uneven and sometimes confusing work.

257 Lapsley, Gaillard. 'Some recent advances in English constitutional history (before 1485)', *Camb. Hist. J.*, 5 (1936), 119–61. Good bibliographical survey.

258 Lyon, Bryce D. *A constitutional and legal history of medieval England.* New York, 1960. A solid introductory account.

259 Maitland, Frederic W. *Constitutional history of England.* Cambridge, 1908.

260 Mitteis, Heinrich. *Lehnrecht und Staatsgewalt.* Weimar, 1933. Useful for putting English developments in a wider medieval perspective.

261 —— *Der Staat des hohen Mittelalters.* Weimar, 1944. An important effort at comparative constitutional history, still basic for Germany, useful for France, but largely unreliable for England, for which Stubbs (269) is his chief source.

262 Morris, William A. *Constitutional history of England to 1216.* New York, 1930.

263 Petit-Dutaillis, Charles. *Studies and notes supplementary to Stubbs' 'Constitutional history' down to the Great Charter.* Manchester, 1908–29, 3 vols.

264 Plucknett, Theodore F. T. *A concise history of the common law.* 5th ed., 1956. The best general work on the subject.

265 Pollock, Frederick and Frederic W. Maitland. *History of English law before the time of Edward I.* 2nd ed., Cambridge, 1898, 2 vols. The great work on the origins and early development of common law. A re-issue with new introduction and select bibliography, 1968, has been announced.

266 Richardson, Henry G. and George O. Sayles. *The governance of mediaeval England from the Conquest to Magna Carta.* Edinburgh, 1963. More fresh insights than are contained in half-a-dozen conventional accounts; but sometimes pushed too hard and stated too categorically.

267 Simpson, Alfred W. B. *Introduction to the history of the land law.* 1961. Good survey.

268 Stenton, Doris M. *English justice between the Norman Conquest and the Great Charter.* Philadelphia, 1964. The fullest account, but see Van Caenegem (247).

269 Stubbs, William. *Constitutional history of England,* vol. I, 6th ed., 1903; vol. II, 4th ed., 1896; vol. III, 5th ed., 1903.

270 Taswell-Langmead, Thomas P. *English constitutional history.* 11th ed., by Theodore F. T. Plucknett. Boston, 1960. Stronger on later periods, but generally useful.

271 Tout, Thomas F. *Chapters in the administrative history of medieval England.* Manchester, 1920–37, 6 vols. The great pioneer work on administrative

history, and still very much a goldmine of information. Vol. I covers the period *c.* 1066–1272.

272 Ullmann, Walter. *The growth of papal government in the middle ages.* 2nd ed., 1962. A misleading title for this immensely learned and provocative book; placed here because of its value in putting Norman monarchy in the perspective of papal ideology on the corporational–juridical nature of the *respublica christiana.*

273 ——— *History of political thought: the middle ages.* Harmondsworth, 1965. A condensation and popularization of (272) and (274).

274 ——— *Principles of government and politics in the middle ages.* 2nd ed., 1966. Pt. I is a condensation and extension of (272); pt. II surveys constitutional development in England and France, but the section on England at least is unsatisfactory, largely because of its misinterpretation of Magna Carta.

275 White, Albert B. *Making of the English constitution.* 2nd ed., New York, 1925.

3 Monographs

276 Adams, George B. *Councils and courts in Anglo-Norman England.* New Haven, 1926.

277 Ault, Warren O. *Private jurisdiction in England,* New Haven, 1923. Standard account.

278 Baldwin, James F. *The king's council in England.* Oxford, 1913. Still the best work on the council, but in need of some updating for the Anglo-Norman period.

279 Bigelow, Melville M. *History of procedure in England from the Norman Conquest; the Norman period 1066–1204.* 1880.

280 Böhmer, Heinrich. *Kirche und Staat in England und in der Normandie im XI. und XII. Jahrhundert.* Leipzig, 1899. Still the basic work on the subject.

281 Cam, Helen M. *The hundred and the hundred rolls.* 1930. Focuses on Edward I, but traces local government back to 1066 for background and continuities.

282 Cantor, Norman. *Church, kingship and lay investiture in England 1089–1135.* Princeton, 1958.

283 Denholm-Young, Noel. *Seignorial administration in England.* Oxford, 1937. Largely devoted to baronial estate management in the thirteenth century, but containing incidental references to the twelfth.

284 Dowell, Stephen. *History of taxation and taxes in England from the earliest times to the present day.* 2nd ed., 1888, 4 vols.

285 Finn, R. Welldon. *The Domesday inquest and the making of Domesday Book.* 1961. An excellent synthesis of Finn's views on the techniques and chronology of the construction of Domesday; cf. (288) and Galbraith (289).

286 ——— *Domesday studies: the eastern counties.* 1967.

287 ——— *Domesday studies: the Liber Exoniensis.* 1964.

288 ——— *Introduction to Domesday Book.* 1963. Basically a follow-up to (285), shifting from how Domesday was constructed to the basic patterns of society it presents.

289 Galbraith, Vivian H. *The making of Domesday Book.* Oxford, 1962. The fullest statement of Galbraith's views on the construction and purposes of Domesday; should be read in conjunction with Finn (285) and (288), as their views tend to dominate present discussion.

290 ——— *Studies in the public records.* Oxford, 1948. Basic work for institutional and administrative history.

291 Goebel, Julius. *Felony and misdemeanor.* New York, 1937. A detailed study of criminal law procedure.

292 Gough, John W. *Fundamental law in English constitutional history.* Oxford, 1955. The early parts of this work, of great importance for the study of seventeenth-century parliamentarians, are of value in placing Norman constitutional development in the perspective, not of institutions, but of an idea.

293 HMSO. *Domesday re-bound.* 2nd ed., 1965. Useful for the physical construction and appearance of Domesday Book.
294 Harcourt, L. W. Vernon. *His Grace the Steward and trial of peers.* 1907.
295 Haskins, Charles Homer. *Norman institutions.* Cambridge, Mass., 1918. The great pioneer work, but superseded in most important respects by now.
296 Holdsworth, William S. *The sources and literature of English law.* Oxford, 1925. A useful introduction.
297 Howell, Margaret. *Regalian right in medieval England.* 1962. Traces the development of regalian right, hardly a problem for England as compared with the continent, to the reign of Edward I.
298 Hoyt, Robert S. *The royal demesne in English constitutional history, 1066–1272.* Ithaca, 1950. A thorough and valuable study.
299 Jolliffe, John E. A. *Angevin kingship.* 2nd ed., 1963. This great work, although devoted to Henry II, Richard I and John, is indispensable for a proper understanding of the dynamics of Norman monarchy as well. Its very style—grim, implacable, oppressive—conveys precisely the qualities of kingship Jolliffe wishes to stress.
300 Joüon des Longrais, Frédéric. *La conception anglaise de la saisine du XIIe au XIVe siècle.* Paris, 1925.
301 Kantorowicz, Ernst H. *Laudes regiae.* Berkeley, 1946. A very important study of the coronation laudes, placing Anglo-Norman practice in its proper European context.
302 Keeton, George W. *The Norman Conquest and the common law.* 1967.
303 Kimball, Elizabeth G. *Serjeanty tenure in medieval England.* New Haven, 1936. The standard account.
304 Lapsley, Gaillard T. *The county palatine of Durham.* New York, 1900. A detailed study of the palatinate from its origins to the nineteenth century; for criticism, see Scammell (414).
305 Larson, Laurence M. *The king's household in England before the Norman Conquest.* Madison, 1904. Useful for comparative purposes.
306 Liebermann, Felix. *Ueber das englische Rechtsbuch Leges Henrici.* Halle, 1901.
307 Lyon, Bryce D. and Adriaan E. Verhulst. *Medieval finance: a comparison of financial institutions in northwestern Europe.* Bruges and Providence, 1967. A detailed comparative study of financial administration in England, Normandy, and Flanders in the eleventh and twelfth centuries.
308 Madox, Thomas. *The history and antiquities of the exchequer of England.* 2nd ed., 1769, 2 vols. Still of great value.
309 Mitchell, Sydney K. *Taxation in medieval England,* ed. Sidney Painter. New Haven, 1951. The subject treated purely from an administrative point of view.
310 Morris, William A. *The early English county court.* Berkeley, 1926.
311 —— *The frankpledge system.* Cambridge, Mass., 1910.
312 —— *The medieval English sheriff to 1300.* Manchester, 1927. Still the only general account, and very valuable.
313 Murray, Katherine M. E. *The constitutional history of the Cinque Ports.* Manchester, 1935. The standard work.
314 Olesen, Tryggvi J. *The witenagemot in the reign of Edward the Confessor.* Toronto, 1955. Useful for comparative purposes.
315 Ormerod, George. *The history of the county palatine and city of Chester.* 2nd ed., 1875–82, 3 vols. Largely superseded for the medieval period by Barraclough (835).
316 Pike, Luke Owen. *A constitutional history of the House of Lords.* 1894.
317 Poole, Reginald Lane. *The exchequer in the twelfth century.* Oxford, 1912. The basic account.
318 Richardson, Henry G. and George O. Sayles. *Law and legislation from Aethelberht to Magna Carta.* Edinburgh, 1966. Supplementary to (266).
319 Riess, Ludwig. *The history of the English electoral law in the middle ages.* Cambridge, 1940.
320 Round, J. Horace. *The king's sergeants and officers of state.* 1911.

321 —— *Studies in the Red Book of the exchequer.* 1898. Often a polemic against
Hall (224).
322 Scherrinsky, Harald. *Untersuchungen zum sogennanten Anonymus von York.*
Würzberg, 1940. Similar to Williams (329).
323 Schramm, Percy E. *History of the English coronation.* Oxford, 1937. The
great study of the symbolism and constitutional significance of coronation
ceremonies and oaths.
324 Valin, Lucien. *Le duc de Normandie et sa cour (912–1204).* Paris, 1909.
325 Weinbaum, Martin. *Verfassungsgeschichte Londons 1066–1258.* Stuttgart,
1929.
326 West, Francis. *The justiciarship in England 1066–1232.* Cambridge, 1966. A
valuable general study.
327 White, Albert B. *Self-government at the king's command.* Minneapolis, 1933.
A basic work, largely based on thirteenth-century evidence.
328 Wilkinson, Bertie. *The coronation in history* (Historical Association Pamph-
lets, General Series, no. 23). 1953. Useful as an introduction.
329 Williams, George H. *The Norman Anonymous of 1100 A.D.* Cambridge,
Mass., 1951. A thorough work on the authorship and structure of thought
of the 'Anonymous of York'; cf. also Cantor (282) and Scherrinsky (322).
330 Young, Charles R. *The English borough and royal administration, 1130–1307.*
Durham, N.C., 1961. Generally useful.

4 Biographies

(See also sec. V, pt. 4, and sec. XII, pt. 4, below)

331 Barlow, Frank. *William I and the Norman Conquest.* 1966. An excellent
survey, stressing the personality and role of the Conqueror.
332 Douglas, David C. 'William the Conqueror: duke and king', in Chevallier
(ed.), *Norman Conquest* [see (205)], pp. 47–76. A condensation and popularization of his great biography of William (528).
333 Longuemare, Elie. *L'Eglise et la conquête de l'Angleterre. Lanfranc, moine
bénédictin, conseiller politique de Guillaume le Conquérant.* Caen and Paris,
1902.

5 Articles

334 Adams, George B. 'Anglo-Saxon feudalism', *AHR,* **7** (Oct. 1901), 11–35.
335 Adams, Norma. 'The writ of prohibition to court Christian', *Minnesota
Law Review,* **20** (1936), 272–93.
336 Archer, Thomas A. 'Ranulf Flambard and his sons', *EHR,* **2** (Jan. 1887),
103–12. Superseded by Southern (416).
337 Barlow, Frank. 'Domesday Book: a letter of Lanfranc', *EHR,* **78** (Apr. 1963),
84–9.
338 Barraclough, Geoffrey. 'Law and legislation in medieval England', *LQR,*
56 (Jan. 1940), 75–92. Valuable general survey.
339 Bateson, Mary. 'The laws of Breteuil', *EHR,* **15** (all issues 1900), 73–8,
302–18, 496–523, 754–7; *EHR,* **16** (Jan. and Apr. 1901), 92–110, 332–45.
Of basic importance for its documents and evidence that borough charters
were modelled after Breteuil.
340 Blair, C. H. Hunter. 'The sheriffs of the county of Durham', *Archaeologia
Aeliana,* 4th ser., **22** (1944), 22–82. From 1070 to 1942; corrects the PRO
List (222).
341 —— 'The sheriffs of Northumberland', *Archaeologia Aeliana,* 4th ser.,
20 (1942), 11–90; 4th ser., **21** (1943), 1–92. Similar to (340).
342 Bond, Shelagh. 'The medieval constables of Windsor Castle', *EHR,* **82**
(Apr. 1967), 225–49.
343 Boussard, Jacques. 'Les institutions financières de l'Angleterre au XIIe
siècle', *Cahiers de civilisation médiévale,* **1** (Oct.–Dec. 1958), 475–94.

344 Brooke, Zachary N. 'Pope Gregory VII's demand for fealty from William the Conqueror', *EHR*, 26 (Apr. 1911), 225–38.

345 Brown, R. Allen. 'The Norman Conquest', *TRHS*, 5th ser., 17 (1967), 109–30. Attempts to enhance the significance of the Conquest by emphasizing shortcomings in Anglo-Saxon government; incorporated in (727).

346 Cam, Helen M. 'Early groups of hundreds', in J. Goronwy Edwards, Vivian H. Galbraith, and Ernest F. Jacob (eds.), *Historical essays in honour of James Tait*, Manchester, 1933, pp. 13–26. Reprinted in Helen M. Cam, *Liberties and communities in medieval England*, corrected ed., 1963, pp. 91–106.

347 —— 'The evolution of the medieval English franchise', *Spec.*, 32 (July 1957), 427–42. Of fundamental importance. Reprinted in Helen M. Cam, *Law-finders and law-makers in medieval England*, 1962, pp. 22–43.

348 —— 'Manerium cum hundredo', *EHR*, 47 (July 1932), 353–76. Reprinted in Cam, *Liberties and communities*, pp. 64–90. See (346).

349 Chaplais, Pierre. 'The seals and original charters of Henry I', *EHR*, 75 (Apr. 1960), 260–75.

350 Chew, Helena M. 'The office of escheater in the city of London during the middle ages', *EHR*, 58 (July 1943), 319–30.

351 Cramer, Alice C. 'The Jewish exchequer', *AHR*, 45 (Jan. 1940), 327–37.

352 —— 'The origins and functions of the Jewish exchequer', *Spec.*, 16 (Apr. 1941), 226–9.

353 Cronne, Henry A. 'The office of local justiciar in England under the Norman kings', *University of Birmingham Historical Journal*, 6 (1957), 18–38. Of great importance for local administration; cf. Reedy (404).

354 —— 'The Salisbury Oath', *Hist.*, new ser., 19 (Dec. 1934), 248–52.

355 Darlington, Reginald R. 'The last phase of Anglo-Saxon history', *Hist.*, new ser., 22 (June 1937), 1–13. Important for its assessment of Anglo-Saxon government and society in the eleventh century.

356 Davis, Henry W. C. 'Waldric the chancellor of Henry I', *EHR*, 26 (Jan. 1911), 84–9.

357 Douglas, David C. 'The Domesday survey', *Hist.*, new ser., 21 (Dec. 1936), 249–57. A useful general assessment.

358 —— 'Edward the Confessor, Duke William of Normandy, and the English succession', *EHR*, 68 (Oct. 1953), 526–45. An important study, supporting the basic reliability of William of Jumièges (465) on the promise of succession made to William. For criticism, see Oleson (402).

359 —— 'Odo, Lanfranc, and the Domesday survey', in Edwards *et al.* (eds.), *Essays . . . Tait*, pp. 47–57. See (346).

360 Edwards, J. Goronwy. 'The Normans and the Welsh March', *Proceedings of the British Academy*, 42 (1956), 155–79. Of major importance for the nature of Norman penetration into Wales and the constitutional powers assumed by the marchers.

361 Farrer, William. 'The sheriffs of Lincolnshire and Yorkshire, 1066–1130', *EHR*, 30 (Apr. 1915), 277–85.

362 Finn, R. Welldon. 'The construction of the Exeter Domesday', *BJRL*, 41 (Mar. 1959), 360–87.

363 —— 'The evolution of successive versions of Domesday Book', *EHR*, 66 (Oct. 1951), 561–4. Argues that the Domesday text was drawn not from original returns, but from local rearrangements of the returns.

364 —— 'The immediate sources of the exchequer Domesday', *BJRL*, 40 (Sept. 1957), 47–78. An elaboration and refinement of the argument in (363).

365 —— 'The Inquisitio Eliensis re-considered,' *EHR*, 75 (July 1960), 385–409.

366 Fliche, Augustin. 'Y a-t-il en France et en Angleterre une querelle des investitures ?', *Revue bénédictine*, 46 (1934), 283–95.

367 Galbraith, Vivian H. 'The date of the geld rolls in Exon Domesday', *EHR*, 65 (Jan. 1950), 1–17. Supports a 1086 date. See also Mason (394).

368 —— 'An episcopal land-grant of 1085', *EHR*, 44 (July 1929), 353–72.

369 —— 'Girard the chancellor', *EHR*, 46 (Jan. 1931), 77–9.

370 —— 'The making of Domesday Book', *EHR*, **57** (Apr. 1942), 161–77. A major revision of views till then dominated by Round (889), and the germ of Galbraith's own synthesis (289).

371 Hamil, Frederick C. 'Presentment of Englishry and the murder fine', *Spec.*, **12** (July 1937), 285–98.

372 —— 'Wreck of the sea in medieval England', in Arthur E. R. Boak (ed.), *University of Michigan historical essays*, Ann Arbor, 1937, pp. 1–24.

373 Haskins, Charles Homer. 'The administration of Normandy under Henry I' *EHR*, **24** (Apr. 1909), 209–31. Incorporated in (295).

374 —— 'Normandy under William the Conqueror', *AHR*, **14** (Apr. 1909), 453–76. Incorporated in (295).

375 Hazeltine, Harold D. 'Roman and canon law in the middle ages', in John B. Bury *et al.* (eds.), *The Cambridge Medieval History*, v, Cambridge, 1926, pp. 697–764. A valuable general account.

376 Holtzmann, Walther. 'Zur Geschichte des Investiturstreites', *Neues Archiv der Gesellschaft für ältere deutsche Geschichte*, **50** (1935), 246–319. Contains references to England; cf. Fliche (366).

377 Hoyt, Robert S. 'The nature and origins of the ancient demesne', *EHR*, **65** (Apr. 1950), 145–74. Reprinted as chapter 6 of (298).

378 —— 'Royal taxation and the growth of the realm in medieval England', *Spec.*, **25** (Jan. 1950), 36–48. Taxation as a basis for the growth of 'national' feeling and action.

379 —— 'The terrae occupatae of Cornwall and the Exon Domesday', *Trad.*, **9** (1953), 155–99.

380 Hurnard, Naomi D. 'The Anglo-Norman franchises', *EHR*, **64** (July and Oct. 1949), 289–327, 433–60. Argues that private franchisal jurisdiction in the Anglo-Norman period was not so extensive as to require radical action by later kings to undermine it.

381 —— 'The jury of presentment and the assize of Clarendon', *EHR*, **56** (July 1941), 374–410.

382 Jenkinson, Hilary. 'The study of English seals', *Journal of the British Archaeological Association*, 3rd ser., **1** (1937), 93–127.

383 Johnson, Charles. 'Waldric, the chancellor of Henry I', *EHR*, **51** (Jan. 1936), 103–4.

384 Jolliffe, John E. A. 'The Domesday hidation of Sussex and the Rapes', *EHR*, **45** (July 1930), 427–35.

385 —— 'The hidation of Kent', *EHR*, **44** (Oct. 1929), 612–18.

386 Lapsley, Gaillard T. 'Mr. Jolliffe's construction of early constitutional history', *Hist.*, new ser., **23** (June 1938), 1–11. Highly critical of Jolliffe (256).

387 Lennard, Reginald V. 'A neglected Domesday satellite', *EHR*, **58** (Jan. 1943), 32–41

388 —— 'The origin of the fiscal carucate', *EcHR*, 1st ser., **14** (Sept. 1944), 51–63. Mainly Anglo-Saxon.

389 Le Patourel, John. 'The date of the trial on Penenden Heath', *EHR*, **61** (Sept. 1946), 378–88. Shows that no precise date can be assigned.

390 —— 'The reports of the trial on Penenden Heath', in Richard W. Hunt, William A. Pantin, and Richard W. Southern (eds.), *Studies in medieval history presented to Frederick Maurice Powicke*, Oxford, 1948, pp. 15–26.

391 Loyn, Henry S. 'The king and the structure of society in late Anglo-Saxon England', *Hist.*, new ser., **42** (June 1957), 87–100. A major (upward) assessment of the vitality of Anglo-Saxon monarchy. See also Darlington (355).

392 McKisack, May. 'London and the succession to the crown during the middle ages', in Hunt *et al.* (eds.), *Studies . . . Powicke* [see (390)], pp. 76–89. Stresses the early and continuous constitutional importance of the Londoners.

393 Maitland, Frederic W. 'English law under Norman and Angevin', in Henry D. Traill and James S. Mann (eds.), *Social England*, 1901–4, 6 vols., I, 398–428.

394 Mason, John F. A. 'The date of the geld rolls,' *EHR*, **69** (Apr. 1954), 283–86. Supports Galbraith (367).

395 Morris, Colin. 'William I and the church courts', *EHR*, **82** (July 1967), 449–63. Denies that William's legislation of 1072–6 provided a full separation of church and royal courts.

396 Morris, William A. 'The lesser *curia regis* under the first two Norman kings of England', *AHR*, **34** (July 1929), 772–8.

397 —— 'The office of sheriff in the early Norman period', *EHR* **33** (Apr. 1918), 145–75. Incorporated in (312).

398 —— 'The sheriffs and the administrative system of Henry I', *EHR*, **37** (Apr. 1922), 161–72. Incorporated in (312).

399 Neilson, Nellie. 'The early pattern of the common law', *AHR*, **49** (Jan. 1944), 199–212.

400 Nineham, Ruth. 'The so-called Anonymous of York', *JEH*, **14** (Apr. 1963), 31–45. A good general account.

401 Odegaard, Charles E. 'Legalis homo', *Spec.*, **15** (Apr. 1940), 186–93. Meaning of the term in the Carolingian age, but applicable later.

402 Oleson, Tryggvi J. 'Edward the Confessor's promise of the throne to Duke William of Normandy', *EHR*, **72** (Apr. 1957), 221–8. Takes issue with Douglas (358).

403 Poole, Reginald Lane. 'The publication of great charters by the English kings', *EHR*, **28** (July 1913), 444–53. Reprinted in Poole, *Studies in chronology and history*, pp. 308–18. See (115).

404 Reedy, William T., Jr. 'The origins of the general eyre in the reign of Henry I', *Spec.*, **41** (Oct. 1966), 688–724. An important study, arguing that the 'general' eyre did not exist, as was urged especially in Richardson and Sayles (266); cf. also Cronne (353).

405 Richardson, Henry G. 'The coronation in medieval England', *Trad.*, **16** (1960), 111–202. An important work, often differing with Schramm (323) and others.

406 —— 'The English coronation oath', *TRHS*, 4th ser., **23** (1941), 129–58. Basically important for the coronation oath of Edward II.

407 —— 'Henry I's charter to London', *EHR*, **42** (Jan. 1927), 80–7.

408 Richardson, Henry G. and George O. Sayles. 'Early coronation records', *BIHR*, **13** (Feb. 1936), 129–45; *BIHR*, **14** (June 1936), 1–9.

409 Riess, Ludwig. 'The re-issue of Henry I's coronation charter', *EHR*, **41** (July 1926), 321–31. Attempts to reconstruct the text of the 1101 charter.

410 Round, J. Horace. 'Bernard, the king's scribe', *EHR*, **14** (July 1899), 417–30. An important examination of the Exchequer under Henry I.

411 —— 'The early sheriffs of Norfolk', *EHR*, **35** (Oct. 1920), 481–96.

412 —— 'The hidation of Northamptonshire', *EHR*, **15** (Jan. 1900), 78–86. Follows up his studies on Northamptonshire (904) and (905); critical of Maitland (735).

413 —— 'Regenbold, priest and chancellor', in J. Horace Round, *Feudal England*, 1895, re-issued 1964, pp. 323–9 (re-issue).

414 Scammell, Jean. 'The origin and limitations of the liberty of Durham', *EHR*, **81** (July 1966), 449–73. A valuable corrective to Lapsley (304).

415 Southern, Richard W. 'The place of Henry I in English history', *Proceedings of the British Academy*, **48** (1962), 127–70. A brilliant assessment, stressing Henry's use of patronage and popularization of royal service as a means of upward mobility.

416 —— 'Ranulf Flambard and early Anglo-Norman administration', *TRHS*, 4th ser., **16** (1933), 95–128. Of fundamental importance for Norman monarchical development.

417 Stephenson, Carl. 'Notes on the composition and interpretation of Domesday Book', *Spec.*, **22** (Jan. 1947), 1–15. Critical of Round (889).

418 Tatlock, John S. P. 'The date of Henry I's charter to London', *Spec.*, **11** (Oct. 1936), 461–9.

419 Thorne, Samuel E. 'Livery of seisin', *LQR*, **52** (July 1936), 345–64.

420 Turner, Ralph V. 'The origin of the medieval English jury: Frankish, English, or Scandinavian?', *JBS*, 7 (May 1968), 1–10. Useful survey of scholarship on the question.
421 Ullmann, Walter. 'The development of the medieval idea of sovereignty', *EHR*, 64 (Jan. 1949), 1–33. Largely incorporated in (274).
422 Walker, Curtis H. 'Sheriffs in the pipe roll of 31 Henry I', *EHR*, 37 (Jan. 1922), 67–79.
423 Ward, Paul L. 'The coronation ceremony in medieval England', *Spec.*, 14 (Apr. 1939), 160–78. Corrections to Schramm (323).
424 White, Geoffrey H. 'Financial administration under Henry I', *TRHS*, 4th ser., 8 (1925), 56–78. Still of basic importance on the subject.
425 —— 'The household of the Norman kings', *TRHS*, 4th ser., 30 (1948), 127–55. The basic study.
426 Wigmore, John H. 'Lanfranc, the prime minister of William the Conqueror: was he once an Italian professor of law?', *LQR*, 58 (Jan. 1942), 61–81.
427 Woodbine, George E. 'The language of English law', *Spec.*, 18 (Oct. 1943), 395–436.

V POLITICAL HISTORY

1 Printed Sources

428 ap Ithel, John W. (ed.). *Annales Cambriae* (RS, no. 20). 1860. Of value for Norman–Welsh relations.

429 Barlow, Frank (ed.). *The life of King Edward who rests at Westminster.* 1962. Supersedes the text in Luard (471).

430 Barraclough, Geoffrey (ed.). 'Some charters of the earls of Chester', in Patricia Barnes and Cecil F. Slade (eds.), *A medieval miscellany for Doris Mary Stenton* (Pipe Roll Society, LXXIV, new ser., XXXVI), 1960, pp. 24–43.

431 Birch, Walter de Gray. (ed.). *Chronicle of Croyland Abbey.* Wisbeck, 1883.

432 Blake, Ernest O. (ed.). *Liber Eliensis* (Camden Society, 3rd ser., XCII). 1962. Chronicle to 1169; numerous letters, charters, etc.

433 Bouquet, Martin *et al.* (eds.). *Receuil des historiens des Gaulles et de la France.* Paris, 1737–1904, 24 vols.

434 Brewer, John S. (ed.). *Chronicon monasterii de bello* (Anglia Christiana Society). 1846. Of major importance for the Conquest.

435 Canterbury, Gervase of. *The historical works of Gervase of Canterbury,* ed. William Stubbs (RS, no. 73). 1879–80, 2 vols.

436 Christie, Richard C. (ed.). *Annales Cestriensis* (Lancashire and Cheshire Record Society, XIV), 1887. Chronicle of the abbey of St Werburgh (founded 1093) to 1297.

437 Clark, Cecily (ed.). *The Peterborough chronicle 1070–1154.* Oxford, 1958.

438 Clark, George T. (ed.). *Cartae et alia munimenta quae ad dominium de Glamorgancia pertinent.* 2nd ed., Cardiff, 1910, 6 vols. Of great importance for the Norman penetration of South Wales.

439 Classen, Ernest and Florence E. Harmer (eds.). *An Anglo-Saxon chronicle.* Manchester, 1926. MS 'D' of the Anglo-Saxon Chronicle, to 1079; with addenda to 1130.

440 Coggeshall, Ralph de. *Radulphi de Coggeshall chronicon Anglicanum,* ed. Joseph Stevenson (RS, no. 66). 1875.

441 Cotton, Bartholomew. *Bartholomaei de Cotton historia Anglicana,* ed. Henry R. Luard (RS, no. 16). 1859.

442 Darlington, Reginald R. (ed.). 'Winchecombe annals, 1049–1181', in Barnes and Slade (eds.), *Medieval miscellany . . . Stenton,* pp. 111–37. See (430)

443 Davis, Henry W. C. (ed.). 'Some documents of the anarchy', in Henry II W. C. Davis (ed.), *Essays in history presented to Reginald Lane Poole,* Oxford, 1927, pp. 168–89.

444 Davis, Ralph H. C. (ed.). 'Treaty between William earl of Gloucester and Roger earl of Hereford', in Barnes and Slade (eds.), *Medieval miscellany . . . Stenton* [see (430)], pp. 139–46. Prints and comments on the pact *c.* 1141–43 which followed up the famous treaty between their fathers, printed in Round (534).

445 Diceto, Ralph de. *Radulphi de Diceto opera historica,* ed. William Stubbs (RS, no. 68). 1876, 2 vols. Begins only in 1148; useful mainly for the Angevins.

446 Dodwell, Barbara (ed.). 'Some charters relating to the honour of Bacton', in Barnes and Slade (eds.), *Medieval miscellany . . . Stenton,* pp. 147–65. See (430).

447 Durham, Symeon of. *Symeonis monachis opera omnia,* ed. Thomas Arnold (RS, no. 75). 1882–5, 2 vols. A miscellany; the most important works are a history of the church of Durham to 1144, and a chronicle, continued by John of Hexham to 1153 (458).

448 Eadmer. *Eadmeri historia novorum in Anglia . . . ,* ed. Martin Rule (RS, no. 81). 1884. A basic narrative source. There is an Engl. trans. by Geoffrey Bosanquet, *Eadmer's history of recent events in England,* Philadelphia, 1965.

449 Earle, John and Charles Plummer (eds.). *Two of the Saxon chronicles*

parallel. Oxford, 1892–9, 2 vols. MSS 'A' and 'E' of the Anglo-Saxon Chronicle.

450 Edwards, Edward (ed.). *Liber monasterii de Hyda* (RS, no. 45). 1866. The main Hyde chronicle ends in 1023, but another covering the period 1035–1121 is also printed.

451 Farrer, William. 'An outline itinerary of King Henry the First', *EHR*, 34 (July and Oct. 1919), 303–82, 505–79. Also printed separately, Oxford, 1920. Still useful, although needs correction and amplification by reference to Johnson and Cronne (230).

452 Gaimar, Geffrei. *L'Estoire des Engleis*, ed. Alexander Bell (Anglo-Norman Text Society). Oxford, 1960.

453 Giles, John A. (ed.). *Scriptores rerum gestarum Willelmi Conquestoris* (Caxton Society). 1845. Includes 16 short pieces on the Norman kings.

454 Glastonbury, John of. *Chronica . . .* , ed. Thomas Hearne. Oxford, 1726.

455 Gloucester, Robert of. *The metrical chronicle of Robert of Gloucester*, ed. William A. Wright (RS, no. 86). 1887, 2 vols. Of little value.

456 Guisborough, Walter of. *The chronicle of Walter of Guisborough*, ed. Harry Rothwell (Camden Society, 3rd ser., LXXXIX). 1957. Mainly important for Edward I.

457 Haskins, George L. (ed.). 'A forged charter of William the Conqueror', *Spec.*, 18 (Oct. 1943), 497–8.

458 Hexham, John of. *Historia Iohannis prioris Hagustaldensis ecclesiae*, ed. Thomas Arnold in (447), II, 284–332. An important continuation of Symeon of Durham to 1153.

459 Hexham, Richard of. *Historia de gestis Stephani et de bello standardii*, ed. Richard Howlett in *Chronicles of the reigns of Stephen, Henry II, and Richard I* (RS, no. 82). 1884–9, 4 vols., III, 139–78. An important source for Stephen.

460 Howden, Roger of. *Chronica Rogeri de Houedene*, ed. William Stubbs (RS, no. 51). 1868–71, 4 vols.

461 Huntingdon, Henry of. *Henrici Huntendunensis historia Anglorum*, ed. Thomas Arnold (RS, no. 74). 1879.

462 Johnson, Charles (ed.). 'Some charters of Henry I', in Edwards *et al.* (eds.), *Essays . . . Tait*, pp. 137–42. See (346).

463 Jones, Thomas (ed. and trans.). *Brut y Tywysogyon (Peniarth MS. 20).* Cardiff, 1941–52, 2 vols. The basic literary source for Norman–Welsh relations.

464 —— *Brut y Tywysogyon: Red Book of Hergest version.* Cardiff, 1955. A variant version, occasionally fuller than (463) but lacking that version's continuation. Text and trans. on facing pages.

465 Jumièges, William of. *Gesta Normannorum ducum*, ed. Jean Marx (Société de l'Histoire de Normandie). Rouen, 1914. Of major importance.

466 Leland, John. *De rebus Britannicis collectanea*, ed. Thomas Hearne. Oxford, 1715.

467 Levison, Wilhelm (ed.). 'Die "Annales Lindisfarnenses et Dunelmenses" ', *Deutsches Archiv*, 17 (1961), 447–506. With extensive commentary.

468 Liebermann, Felix (ed.). *Ungedruckte anglo-normannische Geschichtsquellen.* Strassburg, 1879. Eds. of various short monastic annals.

469 Luard, Henry R. (ed.). *Annales monastici* (RS, no. 36). 1864–9, 5 vols. Eds. of 10 monastic annals, the majority unimportant before the thirteenth century. Of value for the Anglo-Norman period are the *Annales de Margam* (1066–1232) and the *Annales de Theokesberia* (1066–1263), both printed in vol. I.

470 —— *Flores historiarum* (RS, no. 95). 1890, 3 vols. Of some curiosity value only.

471 —— *Lives of Edward the Confessor* (RS, no. 3). 1858. Contains 3 lives, the third and most important now better ed., with trans., in Barlow (429).

472 Macray, William Dunn (ed.). *Chronicon abbatiae de Evesham* (RS, no. 29). 1863. Of value for the period.

473 —— *Chronicon abbatiae Rameseiensis* (RS, no. 83). 1886. Of considerable importance.

474 Malmesbury, William of. *The* 'Historia novella' *of William of Malmesbury*, ed. Kenneth R. Potter. 1955. The best ed., with trans., of this basic source.

475 —— *Willelmi Malmesbiriensis monachi de gestis regum Anglorum . . .* , ed. William Stubbs (RS, no. 90). 1887–9, 2 vols. Vol. II has the text of the *De gestis* from 1066 to 1122, plus the *Historia Novella* now superseded by the ed. of Potter (474).

476 Meyer, Paul (ed.). *L'Histoire de Guillaume le Maréchal* (Société de l'Histoire de France). Paris, 1891–1901, 3 vols. The early lines of this poem are of value for events in Stephen's reign.

477 Michel, Francisque (ed.). *Chroniques anglo-normandes*. Rouen, 1836–40, 3 vols.

478 Newburgh, William of. *Historia rerum Anglicarum*, ed. Richard Howlett in *Chronicles . . . Stephen* [see (459)], I, 1–408, II, 409–583. Deals mainly with the Angevin period, but of some value for Stephen.

479 Orderic Vitalis. *Orderici Vitalis . . . historiae ecclesiasticae libri tredecim*, ed. Auguste Le Prévost (Société de l'Histoire de France). Paris, 1838–55, 5 vols. An indispensable source for Norman and English affairs in the eleventh and early twelfth centuries.

480 Paris, Matthew. *Matthaei Parisiensis chronica majora*, ed. Henry R. Luard (RS, no. 57). 1872–83, 7 vols.

481 —— *Matthaei Parisiensis historia Anglorum sive . . . historia minor*, ed. Frederic Madden (RS, no. 44). 1866–9, 3 vols.

482 Poitiers, William of. *Gesta Guillelmi ducis Normannorum et regis Anglorum*, ed. Raymonde Foreville (Classiques de l'Histoire de France). Paris, 1952. Text and French trans. of this important work.

483 Potter, Kenneth R. (ed.). *Gesta Stephani*. 1955. The single most important literary source for Stephen's reign, containing the hitherto lost final portion, unknown to Richard Howlett in his old ed. in *Chronicles . . . Stephen* [see (459)], III, 3–136. This ed. also contains a trans. For the probable author, see Davis (548).

484 Powell, F. York (ed.). 'A northern legend of the English Conquest', *EHR*, 4 (Jan. 1889), 87–9. Trans. of a part of a thirteenth-century Icelandic saga about Edward the Confessor.

485 Raine, James (ed.). *Historiae Dunelmensis scriptores tres* (Surtees Society, IX). 1839. Chronicles and Durham cathedral documents from the late eleventh to the mid-sixteenth century.

486 Rievaulx, Aelred of. *Relatio de standardo*, ed. Richard Howlett in *Chronicles . . . Stephen* [see (459)], II, 181–99. Of importance for the Battle of the Standard, 1138.

487 Salisbury, John of. *The* Historia pontificalis *of John of Salisbury*, Marjorie Morgan Chibnall. 1956. Of importance for European affairs in the years 1148–52. Text and trans.

488 Salter, Herbert E. (ed.). 'The charters of Henry I and Stephen at Lincoln Cathedral', *EHR*, 23 (Oct. 1908), 725–8.

489 Stevenson, Joseph (ed.). *Chronicon monasterii de Abingdon* (RS, no. 2). 1858, 2 vols. Narrative from the mid-tenth century to Richard I.

490 Stevenson, William H. (ed.). 'An inedited charter of Henry I, 1101', *EHR*, 21 (July 1906), 505–9.

491 Thorpe, Benjamin (ed.). *The Anglo-Saxon chronicle* (RS, no. 23). 1861, 2 vols. Superseded by more recent eds. (439, 449, 494), but still useful for certain purposes.

492 Torigny, Robert of. *Chronique de Robert de Torigni . . .* , ed. Léopold Delisle (Société de l'Histoire de Normandie). Rouen, 1872–3, 2 vols. Supersedes the ed. of Richard Howlett in *Chronicles . . . Stephen*, IV, 3–315. See (459).

493 Wace. *Maistre Wace's 'Roman de Rou . . .'*, ed. Hugo Andresen. Heilbronn, 1877–9, 2 vols. Practically valueless for the Conquest; see Round (576).

494 Whitelock, Dorothy (ed.), with David C. Douglas and Susie I. Tucker. *The Anglo-Saxon chronicle: a revised translation*. 1961. The fullest and best trans.

495 Worcester, Florence of. *Florentii Wigorniensis monachi chronicon ex chronicis . . .* ed. Benjamin Thorpe (English Historical Society). 1848–9, 2 vols.

A valuable chronicle to 1117, with continuations to 1141 and to the end of
the thirteenth century. This ed. is textually corrupt and unsatisfactory,
and a new one is planned.
496 Worcester, John of. *The chronicle of John of Worcester, 1118–1146*, ed.
John R. H. Weaver (Anecdota Oxoniensia, Medieval and Modern Series,
XIII). Oxford, 1908. Especially valuable for Stephen.

2 Surveys

497 Adams, George B. *The history of England from the Norman Conquest to
the death of John, 1066–1216*. 1905. Detailed narrative.
498 Brooke, Christopher N. L. *The Saxon and Norman kings*. 1963. Contains
some fresh and arresting insights.
499 Corbett, William J. 'The development of the duchy of Normandy and the
Norman Conquest of England', in *CMH* [see (375)], V, 481–520. Of
major importance for its discussion of Domesday, and still valuable in
other respects.
500 —— 'England, 1087–1154', in *CMH*, V, 521–53. See (375).
501 Davis, Henry W. C. *England under the Normans and Angevins*. 13th ed.,
1949.
502 Green, John R. *The Conquest of England*. 1899, 2 vols.
503 Hodgkin, Robert H. *A history of the Anglo-Saxons*. 2nd ed., Oxford, 1939,
2 vols. The best detailed history of Anglo-Saxon England, and very useful
for background, but ends with the reign of Alfred the Great.
504 Lappenberg, Johann M. *History of England under the Norman kings*,
trans. Oxford, 1857.
505 Palgrave, Francis. *History of Normandy and England*. 1851–64, 4 vols.
506 Petit-Dutaillis, Charles. *The feudal monarchy in France and England from the
tenth to the thirteenth century*, trans. 1936. An interesting attempt at a
comparative account, but of limited value for England by now.
507 Ramsay, James H. *Foundations of England*. 1898, 2 vols.

3 Monographs

508 Adam, Robert J. *A Conquest of England*. 1965.
509 Butler, Denis. *1066: the story of a year*. 1966.
510 Dupont, Étienne. *La participation de la Bretagne à la conquête de l'Angleterre
par les Normands*. Paris, 1911.
511 Freeman, Edward A. *History of the Norman Conquest of England*. Oxford,
1867–79, 6 vols. Of very limited value by now.
512 —— *The reign of William Rufus*. Oxford, 1882, 2 vols. The only detailed
study of Rufus, and still useful.
513 Furneaux, Rupert. *Conquest 1066*. 1966.
514 Haskins, Charles Homer. *The Normans in European history*. New York,
1915. Uneven but useful for its scope.
515 Kienast, Walter. *Untertaneneid und Treuvorbehalt in Frankreich und England*.
Weimar, 1952.
516 Körner, Sten. *The battle of Hastings, England, and Europe, 1035–1066*.
Lund, 1964. Basically a detailed criticism of the sources relating to the
Conquest.
517 Liebermann, Felix. *Ueber ostenglischen Geschichtsquellen*. Hannover, 1892.
Source criticism.
518 Linklater, Eric. *Conquest of England*. 1966.
519 Lloyd, Alan. *The year of the Conqueror*. 1966.
520 Powicke, F. Maurice. *The loss of Normandy 1189–1204*. 2nd ed., Manchester,
1961. Contains much valuable material on Normandy in the early twelfth
century.
521 Ritchie, R. L. Graeme. *The Normans in England before Edward the Confessor*.
Exeter, 1948. Important for early contacts.

522 Round, J. Horace. *The commune of London and other studies*. Westminster, 1899.

4 Biographies

(*See also sec. IV, pt. 4, above, and sec. XII, pt. 4, below*)

523 Boivin-Champeaux, Louis. *Notice sur Roger le Grand, évêque de Salisbury*. Évreux, 1878.
524 Boüard, Michel de. *Guillaume le Conquérant*. Paris, 1958.
525 Cronne, Henry A. 'Ranulf de Gernons, earl of Chester, 1129–53', *TRHS*, 4th ser., 20 (1937), 103–34. An important study for the politics of Stephen's reign.
526 David, Charles W. *Robert Curthose, duke of Normandy*. Cambridge, Mass., 1920. Very useful in understanding politics in Normandy in the early twelfth century.
527 Davis, Ralph H. C. *King Stephen 1135–1154*. Berkeley, 1967. An excellent political biography and a major contribution to Anglo-Norman studies in general.
528 Douglas, David C. *William the Conqueror*. Berkeley, 1964. A truly great achievement, synthesizing Douglas's article studies and providing a modern, thorough account of Normandy as much as England.
529 Le Patourel, John. 'Geoffrey of Montbray, bishop of Coutances, 1049–1093', *EHR*, 59 (May 1944), 129–61. An important study of one of the Conqueror's leading associates.
530 Onslow, Richard W. A. *The Empress Maud*. 1939. Political biography of Henry I's daughter, but thin.
531 Painter, Sidney. *William Marshal*. Baltimore, 1933. Chapter 1 is useful for the activities of William's father under Stephen.
532 Prentout, Henri. *Histoire de Guillaume le Conquérant*. Caen, 1936. On William as duke of Normandy.
533 Rössler, Oskar. *Kaiserin Mathilde*. Berlin, 1897.
534 Round, J. Horace. *Geoffrey de Mandeville*. 1892. A major study, the nearest Round ever came to a traditional large-scale work. Stresses the venality of the earls under Stephen, but his views have been convincingly modified by Davis (527).
535 Scammell, Geoffrey V. *Hugh de Puiset, bishop of Durham*. Cambridge, 1956. A lively, entertaining account; Hugh was bishop from 1153–95, but the early portions are valuable.
536 Stenton, Frank M. *William the Conqueror and the rule of the Normans*. 1908. Still useful, although now largely superseded by Douglas (528).
537 Waters, Robert E. C. *Gundrada de Warrenne . . .* Exeter, 1884. Essentially a pamphlet, proving she was not the daughter of the Conqueror. See Freeman (557).
538 White, Geoffrey H. 'The career of Waleran, count of Meulan and earl of Worcester'. *TRHS*, 4th ser., 17 (1934), 19–48. The career of an important adherent of Matilda.

5 Articles

539 Baring, Francis H. 'The Conqueror's footprints in Domesday', *EHR*, 13 (Jan. 1898), 17–25. Traces William's itinerary in 1066 through the evidence of Domesday Book.
540 Barlow, Frank. 'The "Carmen de Hastingae proelio" ', in Kenneth Bourne and Donald C. Watt (eds.), *Studies in international history: essays presented to W. Norton Medlicott*, 1967, pp. 35–67. Supports the traditional ascription of the poem, printed in Giles (453), to Guy, bishop of Amiens, and comments on its value as a source for the Conquest.
541 —— 'The *Vita Aedwardi* (Book II); the seven sleepers', *Spec.*, 40 (July

1965), 385–97. Source criticism on the growth of the legend of Edward the Confessor.

542 Barrow, Geoffrey W. S. 'King David and the honour of Lancaster', *EHR*, **70** (Jan. 1955), 85–9. Shows David to have been earl by 1141, not 1147 as argued by Cronne (544).

543 Brooke, Zachary N. and Christopher N. L. Brooke. 'Henry II, duke of Normandy and Aquitaine', *EHR*, **61** (Jan. 1946), 81–9. On Henry's assumption of the titles in 1150 and 1153.

544 Cronne, Henry A. 'The honour of Lancaster in Stephen's reign', *EHR*, **50** (Oct. 1935), 670–80. Cf. Barrow (542).

545 Davis, Henry W. C. 'The anarchy of Stephen's reign', *EHR*, **18** (Oct. 1903), 630–41. Emphasizes the losses to the government, even after the supposed 'normalization' in 1148.

546 —— 'The chronicle of Battle Abbey', *EHR*, **29** (July 1914), 426–34. Source criticism of the chronicle ed. by Brewer (434).

547 —— 'Henry of Blois and Brian Fitz-Count', *EHR*, **24** (Apr. 1910), 297–303.

548 Davis, Ralph H. C. 'The authorship of the "Gesta Stephani"', *EHR*, **77** (Apr. 1962), 209–32. Attributes authorship to Robert of Lewes, bishop of Bath and Wells. See Potter's ed. (483).

549 —— 'Geoffrey de Mandeville reconsidered', *EHR*, **79** (Apr. 1964), 299–307. A reassessment of his political behaviour, taking issue with Round (534).

550 —— 'King Stephen and the earl of Chester revised', *EHR*, **75** (Oct. 1960), 654–60. A reassessment of comital venality stressed by Round (534); expressed more fully in (527).

551 Douglas, David C. 'The ancestors of William fitz Osbern', *EHR*, **59** (Jan. 1944), 62–79.

552 —— '"Companions of the Conqueror"', *Hist.*, new ser., **28** (Sept. 1943), 129–47. Identification of William's associates.

553 —— 'The earliest Norman counts', *EHR*, **61** (Apr. 1946), 129–56. Very important for the origins and growth of those families directly associated with the Conquest.

554 —— 'Les réussites normandes (1050–1100)', *Revue historique*, **237** (Jan.–Mar. 1967), 1–16. Good general survey.

555 Foreville, Raymonde. 'Guillaume de Jumièges et Guillaume de Poitiers', in [Fécamp Abbey] *Ouvrage scientifique du XIIIe centenaire du abbaye de Fécamp*, Fécamp, 1958, pp. 643–53. Comparative source criticism.

556 Fox, Levi. 'The honour and earldom of Leicester', *EHR*, **54** (July 1939), 385–402.

557 Freeman, Edward A. 'The parentage of Gundrada, wife of William of Warren', *EHR*, **3** (Oct. 1888), 680–701. An early argument on her parentage, anticipating the proofs of Waters (537).

558 Galbraith, Vivian H. 'Good kings and bad kings in medieval English history', *Hist.*, new ser., **30** (Sept. 1945), 119–32. A witty and illuminating essay.

559 Jeulin, Paul. 'La consistance du "comté" de Richmond en Angleterre', *Annales de Bretagne*, **44** (1937), 250–78.

560 —— 'Un grand "honneur" anglais. Aperçus sur le "comté" de Richmond en Angleterre, possession des ducs de Bretagne (1069/71–1398)', *Annales de Bretagne*, **42** (1935), 265–302.

561 Le Patourel, John. 'The Plantagenet dominions', *Hist.*, new ser., **50** (Oct. 1965), 289–308. Although devoted to the later twelfth and thirteenth centuries, this study is basic for the Anglo-Norman period as well, for it is the best demonstration that throughout the middle ages, English history is 'provincial history'.

562 Marx, Jean. 'Guillaume de Poitiers et Guillaume de Jumièges', in *Mélanges d'histoire du Moyen Age offerts à M. Ferdinand Lot*, Paris, 1925, pp. 543–8. Comparative criticism and evaluation; cf. Foreville (555).

563 Mason, John F. A. 'The companions of the Conqueror: an additional name', *EHR*, **71** (Jan. 1956), 61–9.

564 —— 'Roger de Montgomery and his sons (1067–1102)', *TRHS*, 5th ser.,

23

13 (1963), 1–28. Very important study of the political activities of this great family.

565 Painter, Sidney. 'The rout of Winchester', *Spec.*, **7** (Jan. 1932), 70–5. Revaluation of the battle of 1141.

566 Parker, Francis H. M. 'The forest laws and the death of William Rufus', *EHR*, **27** (Jan. 1912), 26–38.

567 Patterson, Robert B. 'William of Malmesbury's Robert of Gloucester: a re-evaluation of the *Historia novella*', *AHR*, **70** (July 1965), 983–97. A (downward) assessment of William as an impartial and reliable source.

568 Poole, Austin Lane. 'Henry Plantagenet's early visits to England', *EHR*, **47** (July 1932), 447–52. Henry's visits before 1154.

569 Round, J. Horace. 'The alleged destruction of Leicester', in *FE*, pp. 347–8. See (413).

570 —— 'The alleged invasion of England in 1147', in *FE*, pp. 373–6. See (413).

571 —— 'A charter of Henry I (1123)', *EHR*, **8** (Jan. 1893), 80–3. The earliest mention of the comital title of Robert of Gloucester. Reprinted in *FE*, pp. 366–9. See (413).

572 —— 'The Conqueror at Exeter', in *FE*, pp. 330–46. See (413).

573 —— 'Ely and her despoilers',*"* in *FE*, pp. 349–50. See (413).

574 —— 'King Stephen and the earl of Chester', *EHR*, **10** (Jan. 1895), 87–91. Stresses venality of Ranulf de Gernons; cf. Cronne (525) and Davis (550).

575 —— 'The legend of "Eudo Dapifer" ', *EHR*, **37** (Jan. 1922), 1–34.

576 —— 'Master Wace', in *FE* [see (413)], pp. 306–20. Contemptuous of Wace and anyone who uses him; see also (580) and (1256).

577 —— 'Nigel, bishop of Ely', *EHR*, **8** (July 1893), 515–19.

578 —— 'Normans under Edward the Confessor', in *FE*, pp. 247–57. See (413).

579 —— 'Twelfth century notes', *EHR*, **5** (Oct. 1890), 745–53. Includes notes on one of Henry I's mistresses, the rebel Robert of Bampton under Stephen, and the alleged invasion of 1147, reprinted in *FE*. See (570).

580 —— 'Wace and his authorities', *EHR*, **8** (Oct. 1893), 677–83. A devastating attack on Wace's credibility as a source; cf. also (1256).

581 —— 'Waldric, warrior and chancellor', in *FE*, pp. 364–5. See (413).

582 —— 'Walter Tirel and his wife', in *FE* [see (413)], pp. 255–63. Of basic importance for the assassination of Rufus.

583 Stenton, Frank M. 'The historical background', in Frank M. Stenton (ed.), *The Bayeux tapestry*, 2nd ed., 1965, pp. 9–24.

584 —— 'St. Benet of Holme and the Norman Conquest', *EHR*, **37** (Apr. 1922), 225–35.

585 Strayer, Joseph. 'The development of feudal institutions', in Marshall Clagett *et al.* (eds.), *Twelfth-century Europe and the foundations of modern society*, Madison, 1961, pp. 77–88. A most useful comparative discussion stressing centripetal political tendencies.

586 Walker, David. 'The "honours" of the earls of Hereford in the twelfth century', *Transactions of the Bristol and Gloucestershire Archaeological Society*, **79** (1960–1), 174–211.

587 —— 'Miles of Gloucester, earl of Hereford', *Transactions of the Bristol and Gloucestershire Archaeological Society*, **77** (1958–9), 66–84. Both this and (586) are supplementary to his ed. of Hereford charters (720).

588 White, Geoffrey H. 'Companions of the Conqueror', *Genealogists' Magazine*, **9** (Sept. 1944), 417–24. See also Douglas (552).

589 —— 'The first house of Bellême', *TRHS*, 4th ser., **22** (1940), 67–99. See also Mason (564).

590 —— 'King Stephen's earldoms', *TRHS*, 4th ser., **13** (1930), 51–82.

591 Wightman, Wilfrid E. 'The palatine earldom of William fitz Osbern in Gloucestershire and Worcestershire', *EHR*, **77** (Jan. 1962), 6–17. The earldom from its creation in 1066 to its suppression in 1071.

592 Wilkinson, Bertie. 'Northumbrian separatism in 1065 and 1066', *BJRL*, **23** (Oct. 1939), 504–26. Important for the immediate political antecedents of the Conquest.

VI FOREIGN RELATIONS

1 Printed Sources

593 Anderson, Alan O. (ed.). *Early sources of Scottish history.* 1922, 2 vols.
594 Bain, Joseph (ed.). *Calendar of documents relating to Scotland,* I, *1108–1272.* Edinburgh, 1881.
595 Barrow, Geoffrey W. S. (ed.). *Acts of Malcolm IV, king of Scots, 1153–1165 (Regesta regum Scottorum,* vol. I). Edinburgh, 1960. With excellent critical notes.
596 Bremen, Adam of. *Gesta magistri Adami Hammenburgensis ecclesiae pontificum,* ed. Johann M. Lappenberg (Monumenta Germaniae Historica). 2nd ed., Hannover, 1876. Useful for the activities of English monks in Denmark.
597 Champollion-Figeac, Jacques J. (ed.). *Lettres de Rois, Reines et autres personnages des cours de France et d'Angleterre.* Paris, 1839–47, 2 vols.
598 HMSO. *Diplomatic documents,* vol. I, ed. Pierre Chaplais. 1963. From 1101–1272; only 2 documents for the Anglo-Norman period, but the texts are superior to Rymer (239).
599 —— *List of diplomatic and Scottish documents and papal bulls* (PRO Lists and Indexes, no. 49). 1923.
600 Langlois, Charles V. and Henri Stein (eds.). *Les archives de l'histoire de France.* Paris, 1891–1903, 2 vols.
601 Lawrie, Archibald C. (ed.). *Early Scottish charters prior to A.D. 1153.* Glasgow, 1905.
602 Luchaire, Achille (ed.). *Études sur les actes de Louis VII.* Paris, 1885.
603 —— *Louis VI le Gros. Annales de sa vie et de son règne (1081–1137).* Paris, 1890.
604 Molinier, Auguste. *Les sources de l'histoire de France,* vol. I. Paris, 1901. Covers the period to 1494.
605 Prou, Maurice (ed.). *Recueil des actes de Philippe Ier.* Paris, 1908.
606 Soehnée, Frédéric (ed.). *Catalogue des actes d'Henri Ier.* Paris, 1907.
607 Suger. *Vie de Louis le Gros,* ed. Henri Waquet (Classiques de l'Histoire de France). Paris, 1929.

2 Surveys

608 Ganshof, François. *Histoire des relations internationales: le moyen âge.* 3rd ed., Paris, 1964. Basically only a very good political survey, since 'international relations' in any modern sense did not exist.

3 Monographs

609 Chalandon, Ferdinand. *Histoire de la domination normande en Italie et en Sicile 1009–1194.* Paris, 1907, 2 vols. Useful for diplomatic contacts with Norman England.
610 Dept, Gaston. *Les influences anglaise et française dans le comté de Flandre.* Paris, 1928. Stresses Anglo-French economic rivalries.
611 Dickinson, William C. *A new history of Scotland,* I, *Earliest times to 1603.* 2nd ed., Edinburgh, 1965. The best modern general history, and useful for contacts with England.
612 Fliche, Augustin. *Le règne de Philippe Ier, roi de France.* Paris, 1912.
613 Halphen, Louis. *Le comté d'Anjou au XIe siècle.* Paris, 1906.
614 Kienast, Walter. *Die deutschen Fürsten im Dienste der Westmächte.* Utrecht, Leipzig and Munich, 1924–31, 2 vols.
615 La Chauvelaye, Jules. *Les guerres des Français et des Anglais du XIe au XVe siècle.* Moulins, 1875, 2 vols. A modern, comprehensive work is badly needed.

616 Lloyd, John E. *History of Wales from the earliest times to the Edwardian conquest*. 3rd ed., 1939, 2 vols. The standard authority on early Welsh history, of great value for its information on the political and 'diplomatic' contacts between Welsh and Normans.

617 Lyon, Bryce D. *From fief to indenture*. Cambridge, Mass., 1957. The comprehensive study of the *fief-rente*; shows the diplomatic uses to which it was put by English kings, along with its later development as a military and social institution.

618 Mackie, John D. *History of Scotland*. Harmondsworth, 1964.

619 Pacaut, Marcel. *Louis VII et son royaume*. Paris, 1964. See also Luchaire (602).

620 Rait, Robert S. *An outline of the relations between England and Scotland, 500–1707*. 1901.

621 Ritchie, R. L. Graeme. *The Normans in Scotland*. Edinburgh, 1954. The best general study of early Norman contacts with, and influences in, Scotland.

622 Runciman, Steven. *History of the crusades*, vol. I. Cambridge, 1951. The standard political account, and of value for information on English participation.

623 Sturler, Jean V. *Les relations politiques et des échanges commerciaux entre le duché de Brabant et l'Angleterre au moyen âge*. Paris, 1936.

624 Thompson, James W. *The development of the French monarchy under Louis VI le Gros*. Chicago, 1895. Better treated in Luchaire (603).

625 Toll, Johannes M. *Englands Beziehungen zu den Niederlanden bis 1154*. Berlin, 1921.

626 Tout, Thomas F. *France and England: their relations in the middle ages and now*. Manchester, 1922.

627 Varenbergh, Émile. *Histoire des relations diplomatiques entre le comté de Flandre et l'Angleterre au moyen âge*. Brussels, 1874.

4 Articles

628 Dhondt, Jan. 'Les relations entre la France et Normandie sous Henri I', *Normannia*, 12 (1939), 465–86. For the development of William the Conqueror's position in Normandy prior to the Conquest.

629 Grierson, Philip. 'The relations between England and Flanders before the Norman Conquest', *TRHS*, 4th ser., 23 (1941), 71–112.

630 Halphen, Louis. 'France in the eleventh century', in John B. Bury *et al.* (eds.), *The Cambridge Medieval History*, III, Cambridge, 1922, pp. 99–133.

631 —— 'France: Louis VI and Louis VII (1108–1180)', in *CMH* [see (375)], V, 592–623. Useful for information on contacts with England.

632 Haskins, Charles Homer. 'England and Sicily in the twelfth century', *EHR*, 26 (July and Oct. 1911), 433–47, 641–65. Largely incorporated in (514).

633 Jamison, Evelyn M. 'The Sicilian Norman kingdom in the mind of Anglo-Norman contemporaries', *Proceedings of the British Academy*, 24 (1938), 237–85. Devoted mainly to the Angevin period.

634 Jeulin, Paul. 'L'hommage de la Bretagne en droit et dans le fait', *Annales de Bretagne*, 41 (1934), 380–473. Detailed study of Norman suzerainty over Brittany and the larger Anglo-French entanglements.

635 King, Peter. 'English influence on the church at Odense in the early middle ages', *JEH*, 13 (Oct. 1962), 145–55. English political–religious contacts with Denmark.

636 Leyser, Karl. 'England and the empire in the early twelfth century', *TRHS*, 5th ser., 10 (1960), 61–83. The best treatment of Anglo-German relations in the age of Henry I, from the point of view of the Emperors; contains valuable references for further bibliographical information.

637 Lyon, Bryce D. 'The money fief under the English kings, 1066–1485', *EHR*, 66 (Apr. 1951), 161–93. An early statement of (617).

638 Prestage, Edgar. 'The Anglo-Portuguese alliance', *TRHS*, 4th ser., **17** (1934), 69–100. A detailed survey, from the initial contacts in 1147.

639 Renouard, Yves. 'Essai sur le rôle de l'Empire angevin dans la formation de la France et de la civilisation français aux XIIe et XIIIe siècles', *Revue historique*, **195** (Oct.–Dec. 1945), 289–304. A general interpretation, but containing lines of approach of value for the Anglo-Norman period.

640 Vercauteren, Lina. 'Étude sur les rapports politiques de l'Angleterre et de la Flandre sous le règne du comte Robert II, 1093–1111', in *Études d'histoire dediées à la mémoire de Henri Pirenne*, Brussels, 1937, pp. 413–23.

VII SOCIAL HISTORY

1 Printed Sources

(See also pt. 1 of secs. VIII, IX, and XII, below)

641 Abrahams, Israel and Herbert Loewe (eds.). *Starrs and Jewish charters preserved in the British Museum* (Jewish Historical Society of England). 1930–2, 3 vols.

642 Allen, Percy S. and H. William Garrod (eds.). *Merton muniments* (Oxford Historical Society, LXXXVI). Oxford, 1928. Twelfth-century charters and deeds, with plates.

643 Anderson, Olof S. *The English hundred names*. Lund, 1934.

644 —— *The English hundred-names: the south-eastern counties*. Lund, 1939.

645 —— *The English hundred-names: the south-western counties*. Lund, 1939.

646 Armstrong, Aileen M. *et al. The place-names of Cumberland* (E.P.-N.S., XX–XXII). Cambridge, 1950–2, 3 vols.

647 Baddeley, W. St. Clair. *The place-names of Gloucestershire*. Gloucester, 1913.

648 Bannister, Arthur T. *The place-names of Herefordshire*. Hereford, 1916.

649 Barraclough, Geoffrey (ed.). *Facsimiles of early Cheshire charters* (Lancashire and Cheshire Record Society, CVII). Preston, 1957.

650 Bridgeman, Charles G. O. (ed.). *Staffordshire pre-Conquest charters* (in William Salt Archaeological Society, 3rd ser., vol. for 1916). 1918.

651 Brown, William, Charles T. Clay, *et al.* (eds.). *Yorkshire deeds* (Yorkshire Archaeological Society, Record Series, XXXIX–). 1909–.

652 Cameron, Kenneth. *The place-names of Derbyshire* (E.P.-N.S., XXVII–XXIX). Cambridge, 1959, 3 vols.

653 Charles, Bertie G. *Non-Celtic place-names in Wales*. 1938.

654 Cornford, Margaret E. and E. B. Miller (eds.). *Calendar of the manuscripts in the William Salt Library, Stafford* (in William Salt Archaeological Society, 3rd ser., vol. for 1921). 1921.

655 Douglas, David C. (ed.). 'A charter of enfeoffment under William the Conqueror', *EHR*, **42** (Apr. 1927), 245–7.

656 —— 'Some early surveys from the abbey of Abingdon', *EHR*, **44** (Oct. 1929), 618–25.

657 Dugdale, William. *The baronage of England*. 1675–76, 2 vols. Still of great value as a reference.

658 Ekwall, B. O. Eilert. *English river-names*. Oxford, 1928.

659 —— *The place-names of Lancashire* (Chetham Society, new ser., LXXXI). Manchester, 1922.

660 —— *Street-names of the city of London*. Oxford, 1954.

661 Ellis, Henry J. and Francis B. Bickley (eds.). *Index to the charters and rolls in the department of manuscripts* (of the British Museum). 1900–12, 2 vols.

662 Eyton, Robert W. and George Wrottesley (eds.). *The Staffordshire cartulary* (William Salt Archaeological Society, II, pt. I, III, pt. I). 1881–2, 2 vols.

663 Farrer, William (ed.). *Lancashire pipe rolls . . . and . . . early Lancashire charters . . .* Liverpool, 1902.

664 Farrer, William and Charles T. Clay (eds.). *Early Yorkshire charters* (Yorkshire Archaeological Society, Record Series, Extra Series). Edinburgh and Wakefield, 1914–65, 12 vols. The great collection for the descent of fees in the northern counties.

665 Fowler, G. Herbert (ed.). *The shire of Bedford and the earldom of Huntingdon* (Bedfordshire Historical Record Society, IX). Bedford, 1925. Collection of twelfth-century charters.

666 Fowler, G. Herbert and John G. Jenkins (eds.). *Early Buckinghamshire charters* (Buckinghamshire Record Society Publications, III). Jordans, 1939. Mainly twelfth and thirteenth centuries.

667 Gale, Roger (ed.). *Registrum honoris de Richmond.* 1722.

668 Gelling, Margaret. *The place-names of Oxfordshire* (E.P.-N.S., XXIII–XXIV). Cambridge, 1953–4, 2 vols.

669 Gover, John E. B., Allen Mawer and Frank M. Stenton. *The place-names of Devon* (E.P.-N.S., VIII–IX). Cambridge, 1931–2, 2 vols.

670 —— *The place-names of Hertfordshire* (E.P.-N.S., XV). Cambridge, 1938.

671 —— *The place-names of Middlesex, apart from the City of London* (E.P.-N.S., XVIII). Cambridge, 1942.

672 —— *The place-names of Northamptonshire* (E.P.-N.S., X). Cambridge, 1933.

673 —— *The place-names of Nottinghamshire* (E.P.-N.S., XVII). Cambridge, 1940.

674 —— *The place-names of Surrey* (E.P.-N.S., XI). Cambridge, 1934.

675 —— *The place-names of Warwickshire* (E.P.-N.S., XIII). Cambridge, 1936.

676 —— *The place-names of Wiltshire* (E.P.-N.S., XVI). Cambridge, 1939.

677 Grazebrook, George (ed.). *Shenstone charters* (in William Salt Archaeological Society, XVII). 1896.

678 Gretton, Richard H. (ed.). *Burford records.* Oxford, 1920.

679 HMSO. *Descriptive catalogue of ancient deeds in the Public Record Office.* 1890–1915, 6 vols. Many twelfth-century deeds scattered throughout.

680 Harland, John (ed.). *Mamecestre* . . . (Chetham Society, old ser., LIII, LVI, LVIII). Manchester, 1861–2, 3 vols. Charters and deeds relating to the barony, manor and borough of Manchester.

681 Hart, Cyril E. (ed.). *The early charters of Essex: the Norman period* (University of Leicester, Department of English Local History, Occasional Papers, no. 11). Leicester, 1957.

682 Hassall, William O. (ed.). *Wheatley records* (Oxfordshire Record Society, Record Series, XXXVII). Oxford, 1956. A miscellany of translated documents to commemorate the thousandth anniversary.

683 Hervey, Francis (ed.). *Pinchbeck register.* 1925. 2 vols.

684 Hoyt, Robert S. (ed.). 'A pre-Domesday Kentish assessment list', in Barnes and Slade (eds.), *Medieval miscellany . . . Stenton*, pp. 189–202. See (430).

685 Le Patourel, John (ed.). *Documents relating to the manor and borough of Leeds, 1066–1400* (Thoresby Society, XLV). Leeds, 1956.

686 Loyd, Lewis C. and Doris M. Stenton (eds.). *Sir Christopher Hatton's book of seals* (Northamptonshire Record Society, XV). Oxford, 1950. Transcripts and plates of over 500 charters, twelfth to seventeenth centuries.

687 Madox, Thomas. *Baronia Anglica.* 1736. Still useful; cf. Dugdale (657).

688 Map, Walter. *De nugis curialium,* ed. Montague Rhodes James (Anecdota Oxoniensia, 4th ser., XIV). Oxford, 1914. Valuable in reflecting social values and behaviour, especially for the Angevins.

689 Martin, M. T. (ed.). *The Percy cartulary* (Surtees Society, CXVII). Durham, 1911. Mainly fourteenth to sixteenth centuries, but includes a charter of Henry I to Newcastle upon Tyne.

690 Mawer, Allen. *The chief elements used in English place-names* (E.P.-N.S., I, pt. 2). Cambridge, 1924.

691 Mawer, Allen and Frank M. Stenton. *Introduction to the survey of English place-names* (E.P.-N.S., I, pt. 1). Cambridge, 1924.

692 —— *The place-names of Bedfordshire and Huntingdonshire* (E.P.-N.S., III). Cambridge, 1926.

693 —— *The place-names of Buckinghamshire* (E.P.-N.S., II). Cambridge, 1925.
694 —— *The place-names of Sussex* (E.P.-N.S., VI–VII). Cambridge, 1929–30, 2 vols.
695 —— *The place-names of Worcestershire* (E.P.-N.S., IV). Cambridge, 1927.
696 Mellows, William T. (ed.). *Henry of Pytchley's book of fees* (Northamptonshire Record Society, II). Kettering, 1927. Compiled *c.* 1400, relating to fees held of the abbey of Peterborough.
697 Napier, Arthur S. and William H. Stevenson (eds.). *The Crawford collection of early charters and documents* (Anecdota Oxoniensia, Medieval and Modern Series, VII). Oxford, 1895. An important collection.
698 Nichols, John G. *et al. Collectanea topographica et genealogica.* 1834–43, 8 vols.
699 Parker, James (ed.). *The early history of Oxford* (Oxford Historical Society, III). Oxford, 1885. Extensive documents for the period 727–1100.
700 Reaney, Percy H. *The origin of English place names.* 1960.
701 —— *The place-names of Cambridgeshire and the Isle of Ely* (E.P.-N.S., XIX). Cambridge, 1943.
702 —— *The place-names of Essex* (E.P.-N.S., XII). Cambridge, 1935.
703 Riley, Henry T. (ed.). *Munimenta Gildhallae Londoniensis* (RS, no. 12). 1859–62, 3 vols.
704 Round, J. Horace (ed.). *Ancient charters* (Pipe Roll Society, X). 1888. Royal and private charters, *c.* 1095–1200.
705 Salter, Herbert E. (ed.). *Medieval Oxford* (Oxford Historical Society, C). Oxford, 1936.
706 —— *Newington Longeville charters* (Oxfordshire Record Society, Record Series, III). Oxford, 1921.
707 Savage, Henry E. (ed.). *Shenstone charters* (in William Salt Archaeological Society, 3rd ser., vol. for 1923). 1924.
708 Smith, Albert H. *English place-name elements* (E.P.-N.S., XXV–XXVI). Cambridge, 1956, 2 vols.
709 —— *The place-names of the East Riding of Yorkshire and York* (E.P.-N.S., XIV). Cambridge, 1937.
710 —— *The place-names of Gloucestershire* (E.P.-N.S., XXXVIII–XLI). Cambridge, 1964–5, 4 vols.
711 —— *The place-names of the North Riding of Yorkshire* (E.P.-N.S., V). Cambridge, 1928.
712 —— *The place-names of the West Riding of Yorkshire* (E.P.-N.S., XXX–XXXVII). Cambridge, 1961–2, 8 vols.
713 Stenton, Frank M. (ed.). *Documents illustrative of the social and economic history of the Danelaw* (British Academy, Records of the Social and Economic History of England and Wales, no. 5). 1920. Fundamental collection of transcripts of twelfth-century charters.
714 —— *Facsimiles of early charters from Northamptonshire collections* (Northamptonshire Record Society, IV). Kettering, 1930. Lay and ecclesiastical charters, eleventh to thirteenth centuries. Also very useful for paleographical work.
715 Stow, John. *Survey of London*, ed. Charles L. Kingsford. Oxford, 1908, 2 vols. The best ed. of this great antiquarian work.
716 Taylor, Frank (ed.). 'Selected Cheshire seals (12th–17th century) from the collection in the John Rylands Library', *BJRL*, **26** (June 1942), 393–412. Annotated list.
717 Turner, Joseph H. *Yorkshire place-names as recorded in the Yorkshire Domesday Book, 1086 . . .* Bingley, 1900.
718 Turner, William H. (ed.). *Calendar of charters and rolls preserved in the Bodleian Library.* Oxford, 1878.
719 Wagner, Anthony R. (ed.). *Historic heraldry of Britain.* Oxford, 1939.
720 Walker, David (ed.). 'Charters of the earldom of Hereford', in *Camden Miscellany*, **22** (Camden Society, 4th ser., I). 1964, pp. 1–75.
721 Wallenberg, Johannes K. *The place-names of Kent.* Uppsala, 1934.
722 Whitelock, Dorothy (ed.). *Anglo-Saxon wills.* Cambridge, 1930.
723 Wright, Thomas (ed.). *Anglo-Latin satirical poets and epigrammatists of the*

twelfth century (RS, no. 59). 1872, 2 vols. Of use for social values; cf. Map (688).

2 Surveys

724 Barlow, Frank. 'The effects of the Norman Conquest', in Chevallier (ed.), *Norman Conquest* [see (205)], pp. 125–61. A very good general account.
725 Bennett, Henry S. *Life on the English manor. A study of peasant conditions 1150–1450.* Cambridge, 1937. Mainly devoted to later periods, but much of it applicable.
726 Bloch, Marc. *Seigneurie française et manoir anglais.* Paris, 1960. A generalized comparative account, not originally intended for publication.
727 Brown, R. Allan. *The Norman Conquest.* 1969. Stresses social and cultural change.
728 Coulton, George G. *Social life in Britain from the Conquest to the Reformation.* New ed., 1938.
729 —— *Medieval panorama.* Cambridge, 1938. Both this and (728) are potpourris, but useful and entertaining.
730 Darlington, Reginald R. *The Norman Conquest.* 1963. Short general interpretation.
731 Duby, Georges. *L'Économie rurale et la vie des compagnes dans l'occident médiéval.* Paris, 1962, 2 vols. A superb example of comparative social history, putting English developments in their much-needed wider European perspective. An Engl. trans. has appeared (1968).
732 John, Eric. *Land tenure in early England.* Leicester, 1961. A difficult and controversial work, devoted to Anglo-Saxon history but with relevance for the post-Conquest period.
733 Lennard, Reginald V. *Rural England, 1086–1135.* Oxford, 1959. An excellent general account of social and agrarian history.
734 Loyn, Henry R. *Anglo-Saxon England and the Norman Conquest.* 1962. A very good survey of the social and economic history of England to Domesday Book.
735 Maitland, Frederic W. *Domesday Book and beyond.* Cambridge, 1897. One of the masterpieces of English historical literature, attempting to read back from the evidence of Domesday to earlier social structure. For evaluations and criticisms, see Edward Miller's introduction to the Fontana paperback ed., 1960, and Bryce D. Lyon's introduction to the Norton paperback ed., New York, 1966.
736 Medley, Dudley J. 'Social Life', in Traill and Mann (eds.), *Social England* [see (393)], I, 532–58. A thin, superficial essay.
737 Painter, Sidney. *Studies in the history of the English feudal barony.* Baltimore, 1943. A wide-ranging and suggestive study of the baronage as a social class, twelfth to fourteenth centuries.
738 Tomkeieff, Olive G. *Life in Norman England.* 1966.
739 Vinogradoff, Paul. *English society in the 11th century.* Oxford, 1908. Still of value. See also (822) and (823).

3 Monographs

740 Adler, Michael. *The Jews of medieval England.* 1939.
741 Baddeley, W. St. Clair. *History of Cirencester.* Cirencester, 1924.
742 Ballard, Adolphus. *The Domesday inquest.* 1906. A general assessment of social structure as reflected by the evidence of Domesday Book.
743 —— *History of Chichester.* Chichester, 1898.
744 Beresford, Maurice W. and John K. S. St. Joseph. *Mediaeval England: an aerial survey.* Cambridge, 1958. An unusual and fascinating book, demonstrating the value of aerial photography for historical purposes.
745 Billson, Charles J. *Medieval Leicester.* Leicester, 1920.

746 Blomefield, Francis. *An essay towards a topographical history of the county of Norfolk.* Lynn, 1739–75, 5 vols.

747 Bridges, John. *The history and antiquities of Northamptonshire.* Oxford, 1791, 2 vols.

748 Brooke, Iris. *A history of English costume.* 1937.

749 Calthrop, Dion C. *English costume from William I to George IV, 1066–1830.* 1937.

750 Chibnall, Albert C. *Sherington: fiefs and fields of a Buckinghamshire village.* Cambridge, 1965. A model history of its kind, avoiding the pitfalls of antiquarianism and presenting an excellent microcosmic view of social history, from the twelfth to the end of the eighteenth century.

751 Colvin, Howard M. *History of Deddington, Oxfordshire.* 1963. A good social study.

752 Cunningham, William. *Alien immigrants to England.* 1897. Still a basic work on the subject.

753 Davies, Maud F. *Life in an English village: an economic and historical survey of the parish of Corsley in Wiltshire.* 1909.

754 Douglas, David C. *The social structure of medieval East Anglia.* Oxford, 1927. Of fundamental value and importance.

755 Drake, Francis. *Eboracum, or the history and antiquities of the city of York, with the history of the cathedral church.* 1736.

756 Du Boulay, Francis R. H. *Medieval Bexley.* Bexley, 1961. A short, popular but useful account of a Kent community.

757 Ducarel, Andrew C. *Anglo-Norman antiquities.* 1767. One of the better antiquarian compilations, and still of great value.

758 Dugdale, William. *Antiquities of Warwickshire.* 1656.

759 Duncumb, John. *Collections towards the history and antiquities of the county of Hereford.* Hereford, 1804–42, 3 vols.

760 Ekwall, B. O. Eilert. *Studies on English place names.* Stockholm, 1936.

761 —— *Studies on the population of medieval London.* Stockholm, 1956.

762 Elliott-Binns, Leonard E. *Medieval Cornwall.* 1955.

763 Eyton, Robert W. *Antiquities of Shropshire.* 1854–60, 12 vols. Still of much value.

764 —— *Domesday studies: an analysis and digest of the Somerset survey . . .* 1880, 2 vols.

765 —— *Domesday studies: an analysis and digest of the Staffordshire survey . . .* 1881.

766 —— *A Key to Domesday: . . . an analysis and digest of the Dorset survey.* 1878.

767 —— *Notes on Domesday.* Bristol, 1880.

768 Farrer, William. *Feudal Cambridgeshire.* Cambridge, 1920. An important study of the distribution of landholders.

769 Feilitzen, Olof von. *The pre-Conquest personal names of Domesday.* Uppsala, 1937.

770 Finberg, Herbert P. R. *Gloucestershire studies.* Leicester, 1957. Miscellaneous but valuable essays on aspects of local history.

771 —— *Lucerna.* 1964. Collection of essays, mainly Anglo-Saxon but some relevant as late as the mid-twelfth century.

772 Finberg, Herbert P. R. and William G. Hoskins. *Devonshire studies.* 1952.

773 Foster, Charles W. *A history of the villages of Aisthorpe and Thorpe in the Fallows.* Lincoln, 1927. An excellent social study.

774 Fransson, Gustav. *Middle English surnames of occupations, 1100–1350.* Lund, 1935.

775 Gorges, Raymond. *The story of a family through eleven centuries . . .* Boston, 1944.

776 Gras, Norman S. B. and Ethel C. Gras. *The economic and social history of an English village (Crawley, Hampshire) A.D. 909–1928.* Cambridge, Mass., 1930. Especially valuable for its extensive documentation.

777 Gray, Arthur. *The town of Cambridge: a history.* Cambridge, 1925.

778 Hall, Donald J. *English medieval pilgrimage.* 1965.

779 Hemmeon, Morley de Wulf. *Burgage tenure in medieval England*. Cambridge, Mass., 1914. Still a standard account.

780 Hill, James W. F. *Medieval Lincoln*. Cambridge, 1948. An excellent urban history, a model of its kind.

781 Hoare, Richard C. *et al. Modern Wiltshire*. 1822–44, 14 pts.

782 Hodgson, John. *A history of Northumberland*. Newcastle upon Tyne, 1827–58, 6 vols. in 3 pts. Still a valuable antiquarian collection; continued in Bateson (145).

783 Hoskins, William G. *Essays in Leicestershire history*. Liverpool, 1950.

784 —— *The Midland peasant*. 1957. An important study of Wigston Magna, Leics., from the sixth to the nineteenth century.

785 Hutchins, John. *History and antiquities of the county of Dorset*. 3rd ed., 1861–70, 4 vols.

786 Jusserand, Jean A. *English wayfaring life in the middle ages*. 4th ed., 1950. Largely devoted to the fourteenth century.

787 Lobel, Mary D. *The borough of Bury St. Edmunds*. Oxford, 1935. Reliable and useful.

788 Loyd, Lewis C. *The origins of some Anglo-Norman families*, ed. Charles T. Clay and David C. Douglas (Harleian Society, CIII). Leeds, 1951. A major genealogical work, clarifying the pedigrees of most of the great Anglo-Norman noble families.

789 Mason, Robert H. *History of Norfolk*. 1884–5, 5 pts.

790 Morant, Philip. *History and antiquities of Essex*. 1768, 2 vols.

791 Nelson, Lynn H. *The Normans in South Wales 1070–1171*. Austin, 1966. An erratic, disappointing book on a subject of great importance.

792 Nicholls, James F. and John Taylor. *Bristol past and present*. Bristol, 1881–2, 3 vols. Mystifyingly arranged, but of importance for its documents.

793 Nichols, John. *History and antiquities of the county of Leicester*. 1795–1811, 4 vols. in 8 pts.

794 Poole, Austin Lane. *Obligations of society in the twelfth and thirteenth centuries*. Oxford, 1946. Brief but illuminating.

795 Powley, Edward B. *The house of De La Pomerai*. Liverpool, 1944.

796 Raftis, J. Ambrose. *Tenure and mobility*. Toronto, 1964. Mainly devoted to later periods, but the questions it asks are of major importance.

797 Redford, Arthur. *The history of local government in Manchester*, I. 1939.

798 Richardson, Henry G. *The English Jewry under Angevin kings*. 1960. Probably the best work on the subject for any medieval period, and relevant to Anglo-Norman developments.

799 Robinson, J. Armitage. *Somerset historical essays*. 1911. Wide-ranging and important.

800 Robo, Étienne. *Medieval Farnham*. Farnham, 1935.

801 Rogers, Alan *et al. The making of Stamford*. Leicester, 1965.

802 Roth, Cecil, *A history of the Jews in England*. 2nd ed., Oxford, 1949. The standard general account.

803 Round, J. Horace. *Family origins and other studies*, ed. William Page. 1930. Collected studies on genealogy.

804 —— *Peerage and pedigree*. 1910, 2 vols. Collected studies.

805 —— *Studies in peerage and family history*. Westminster, 1901. Collected studies.

806 Russell, Josiah C. *British medieval population*. Albuquerque, 1948. The only large-scale work, and important less for its conclusions than for the developments in demographic analysis it has helped to stimulate.

807 Rye, Walter. *A history of Norfolk*. 1887.

808 Salter, Herbert E. *Survey of Oxford*, ed. William A. Pantin (Oxford Historical Society, new ser., XIV). Oxford, 1960

809 Sharpe, Montagu. *Middlesex in the eleventh century*. Brentford, 1941.

810 Shaw, Stebbing. *History and antiquities of Staffordshire* . . . 1798–1801, 2 vols.

811 Sheehan, Michael M. *The will in medieval England*. Toronto, 1963. A careful and comprehensive study.

812 Sitwell, George. *The barons of Pulford*. Scarborough, 1889.

813 Stenton, Doris M. *The English woman in history.* 1957.
814 Stenton, Frank M. *The first century of English feudalism, 1066–1166.* 2nd ed., Oxford, 1961. The great work on the Anglo-Norman baronage, of fundamental importance for political and institutional as well as social history.
815 —— *Types of manorial structure in the northern Danelaw.* Oxford, 1910. A major work, indicating clearly the variations in social and legal structures occasioned by Scandinavian colonization and settlement.
816 Surtees, Robert. *History and antiquities of the county palatine of Durham.* 1816–40, 4 vols. Largely superseded by Lapsley (304).
817 Taylor, Charles S. *An analysis of the Domesday survey of Gloucestershire.* Bristol, 1889. Still useful for its data.
818 Thompson, James W. *The literacy of the laity in the middle ages.* Berkeley, 1939. Important for showing that lay literacy was wider spread than had hitherto been assumed.
819 Thoroton, Robert. *Thoroton's history of Nottinghamshire.* 2nd ed., 1797, 3 vols.
820 Tierney, Mark A. *The history and antiquities of the castle and town of Arundel.* 1834, 2 vols.
821 Tindal, William. *The history and antiquities of the abbey and borough of Evesham.* Evesham, 1794.
822 Vinogradoff, Paul. *The growth of the manor.* 2nd ed., 1911. Still of value, but needs to be read in the light of Aston (1099).
823 —— *Villainage in England.* Oxford, 1892.
824 Wagner, Anthony R. *English ancestry.* Oxford, 1961. Abridgment of (825).
825 —— *English genealogy.* 1960. A massive and illuminating work, of great value for the question of upward social mobility.
826 —— *Heralds and heraldry in the middle ages.* Oxford, 1939. The standard account.
827 Wheatley, Henry B. *London past and present.* 1891, 3 vols. Still useful potpourri.
828 Whellan, William. *The history and topography of the counties of Cumberland and Westmorland.* Pontefract, 1860.
829 Wightman, Wilfrid E. *The Lacy family in England and Normandy, 1066–1194.* Oxford, 1966. Detailed political and social study of this important family.
830 Williams, Gwyn. *Medieval London.* 1963. Basic modern account of the growth of the commune, but not always convincing on every point.
831 Yeatman, John P. *et al. Feudal history of the county of Derby.* 1886, 2 vols.
832 Zachrisson, Robert E. *A contribution to the study of Anglo-Norman influence on English place names.* Lund, 1909.

4 Articles

833 Ackerman, Robert W. 'The knighting ceremonies in the Middle English romances', *Spec.*, **19** (July 1944), 285–313.
834 Bandel, Betty. 'The English chroniclers' attitude toward women', *JHI*, **16** (Jan. 1955), 113–18.
835 Barraclough, Geoffrey. 'The earldom and county palatine of Chester', *Transactions of the Historic Society of Lancashire and Cheshire*, CIII (1953), 23–57. A basic study of the social and political organization of the palatinate; supersedes Ormerod (315).
836 Barrow, Geoffrey W. S. 'The beginnings of feudalism in Scotland', *BIHR*, **29** (May 1956), 1–31. The best study of the subject.
837 Bishop, Terence A. 'The Norman settlement of Yorkshire', in Hunt *et al.* (eds.), *Studies . . . Powicke*, pp. 1–14. See (390).
838 Bloch, Marc. 'The rise of dependent cultivation and seignorial institutions', in Michael M. Postan (ed.), *The Cambridge economic history of Europe*, I, *The agrarian life of the middle ages*, 2nd ed., Cambridge, 1966, pp. 235–

89. The best starting-point for the problem of the growth of peasant dependence.

839 Cam, Helen M. 'The community of the vill', in Veronica Ruffer (ed.), *Medieval studies presented to Rose Graham*, Oxford, 1950, pp. 1–14. Reprinted in Cam, *Law-finders and law-makers*, pp. 71–84. See (347).

840 —— 'The origin of the borough of Cambridge', *Proceedings of the Cambridge Antiquarian Society*, 35 (1935), 33–53. Reprinted in Cam, *Liberties and communities* [see (346)], pp. 1–18. Detailed criticism of Stephenson (990) based on Cambridge evidence.

841 Coulborn, Rushton. 'A comparative study of feudalism', in Rushton Coulborn (ed.), *Feudalism in history*, Princeton, 1956, pp. 185–395. Highly schematized, unconvincing attempt to posit feudalism as a recurrent social form.

842 Darlington, Reginald R. 'Introduction to Wiltshire Domesday', in (199), II, 42–112.

843 —— 'Introduction to Wiltshire geld rolls', in (199), II, 167–77.

844 Davis, Ralph H. C. 'The Norman Conquest', *Hist.*, new ser., 51 (Oct. 1966), 279–86. General interpretation stressing Norman reliance on Anglo-Saxon institutions.

845 —— 'What happened in Stephen's reign, 1135–1154', *Hist.*, new ser., 49 (Feb. 1964), 1–12. Emphasizes the growth of hereditability of fees, more fully worked out in (527).

846 Dodwell, Barbara. 'East Anglian commendation', *EHR*, 63 (July 1948), 289–306. An important article, arguing that commendation was territorialized and hence permanent although not necessarily personal; supports Maitland (735) as against Stephenson (933).

847 —— 'The free peasantry of East Anglia in Domesday', *Original Papers of the Norfolk and Norwich Archaeological Society*, 28 (1939), 145–57.

848 —— 'Holdings and inheritance in medieval East Anglia', *EcHR*, 2nd ser., 20 (Apr. 1967), 53–66.

849 Donkin, R. A. 'Settlement and depopulation on Cistercian estates during the twelfth and thirteenth centuries, especially in Yorkshire', *BIHR*, 33 (Nov. 1960), 141–65.

850 Douglas, David C. 'The Norman Conquest and English feudalism', *EcHR*, 1st ser., 9 (May 1939), 128–43. Emphasizes the social changes introduced and/or hastened by the Conquest.

851 Du Boulay, Francis R. H. 'Gavelkind and knight's fee in medieval Kent', *EHR*, 77 (July 1962), 504–11.

852 Ekwall, B. O. Eilert. 'Names of trades in English place names', in Edwards et al. (eds.), *Essays . . . Tait*, pp. 79–89. See (346).

853 Farrer, William. 'The feudal baronage', in *VCH Lancaster* (158), I, 291–376.

854 —— 'Introduction to the Lancashire Domesday', in (158), I, 269–82.

855 —— 'Introduction to the Yorkshire Domesday', in (195), II, 133–90.

856 Galbraith, Vivian H. 'Nationality and language in medieval England', *TRHS*, 4th ser., 23 (1941), 113–28.

857 Hill, James W. F. 'Danish and Norman Lincoln', *Associated Architectural Societies' Reports and Papers*, 41 (1932), 7–22.

858 Hilton, Rodney H. 'Freedom and villeinage in England', *PP*, no. 31 (July 1965), 3–19. Stresses access to royal courts.

859 Hodgett, G. A. J. 'Feudal Wiltshire', in (199), v, 44–71.

860 Holt, James C. 'Feudalism revisited', *EcHR*, 2nd ser., 14 (Dec. 1961), 333–40.

861 Homans, George C. 'Men and the land in the middle ages', *Spec.*, 11 (July 1936), 338–51.

862 —— 'Partible inheritance of villagers' holdings', *EcHR*, 1st ser., 8 (Nov. 1937), 48–56.

863 —— 'The rural sociology of medieval England', *PP*, no. 4 (Nov. 1953), 32–43.

864 Hoyt, Robert S. 'Farm of the manor and community of the vill in Domesday Book', *Spec.*, 30 (Apr. 1955), 147–69.

865 John, Eric. 'English feudalism and the structure of Anglo-Saxon society', *BJRL*, **46** (Sept. 1963), 14–41. Argues for a large-scale 'feudal system' before 1066.

866 Johnson, Charles. 'Introduction to the Norfolk Domesday', in (185), II, 1–38.

867 Jolliffe, John E. A. 'Northumbrian institutions', *EHR*, **41** (Jan. 1926), 1–42. Of major importance for the question of regional variations in political and social structure.

868 —— 'The origin of the hundred in Kent', in Edwards *et al.* (eds.), *Essays . . . Tait*, pp. 155–68. See (346).

869 Joüon des Longrais, Frédéric. 'Le vilainage anglais et le servage réel et personnel: quelques remarques sur la période 1066–1485', in *Recueil de la Société Jean Bodin*, Brussels, 1937, pp. 199–242.

870 Koebner, Richard. 'The settlement and colonization of Europe', in *CEH*, I, 1–91. See (838).

871 Lapsley, Gaillard T. 'Introduction to the Boldon Book', in *VCH Durham* (174), I, 259–326. Attempts to read back from the Boldon Book (*c.* 1183) to the Domesday period.

872 Latham, Lucy C. 'The manor and the village', in Geoffrey Barraclough (ed.), *Social life in early England*, 1960, pp. 29–50. Originally published as Historical Association Pamphlet, no. 83. 1931.

873 Le Bras, Gabriel. 'Conceptions of economy and society', in Michael M. Postan, Edwin E. Rich and Edward Miller (eds.), *The Cambridge economic history of Europe*, III, *Economic organization and policies in the middle ages*, Cambridge, 1963, pp. 554–75.

874 Lees, Beatrice A. 'Introduction to the Suffolk Domesday', in (192), I, 357–417.

875 Lennard, Reginald V. 'The economic position of the bordars and cottars of Domesday Book', *Economic Journal*, **61** (June 1951), 342–71.

876 —— 'The economic position of the Domesday sokemen', *Economic Journal*, **57** (June 1947), 179–95.

877 —— 'The economic position of the Domesday *villani*', *Economic Journal*, **56** (June 1946), 244–64.

878 —— 'Peasant tithe-collectors in Norman England', *EHR*, **69** (Oct. 1954), 580–96.

879 Lyon, Bryce D. 'Medieval real estate developments and freedom', *AHR*, **63** (Oct. 1957), 47–61. Relations between reclamation and the decline of seigneurialism; mostly on the Low Countries but suggestive for England.

880 Maitland, Frederic W. 'Northumbrian tenures', *EHR*, **5** (Oct. 1890), 625–32. Stresses the antiquity and regional peculiarities of tenure in the north.

881 Neilson, Nellie. 'Introduction to the Kent Domesday', in (180), III, 177–202.

882 Oakley, Thomas P. 'Penitentials as sources for medieval history', *Spec.*, **15** (Apr. 1940), 210–23.

883 Painter, Sidney. 'The family and the feudal system in twelfth-century England', *Spec.*, **35** (Jan. 1960), 1–16. Important descriptive account of ties of family solidarity.

884 —— 'The house of Quency, 1136–1264', *Medievalia et Humanistica*, no. **11** (1957), 3–9.

885 Pollock, Frederick. 'A brief survey of Domesday', *EHR*, **11** (Apr. 1896), 209–30. General assessment of social structure and agrarian life.

886 Poole, Austin Lane. 'Recreations', in Austin Lane Poole (ed.), *Medieval England*, II, 605–32. See (55).

887 Powell, F. York. 'Domesday Book', in Traill and Mann (eds.), *Social England*, I, 340–49. See (393).

888 Reichel, Oswald J. 'Introduction to the Devonshire Domesday', in (172), I, 375–402.

889 Round, J. Horace. 'Domesday Book', in *FE* [see (413)] pp. 17–123. Round's fullest and most persuasive study; cf. Galbraith (370).

890 —— 'Introduction to the Bedfordshire Domesday', in (167), I, 191–218.

891 —— 'Introduction to the Berkshire Domesday', in (168), I, 285–323.

892 —— 'Introduction to the Buckinghamshire Domesday', in (169), I, 207–29.
893 —— 'Introduction to the Essex Domesday', in (175), I, 333–426.
894 —— 'Introduction to the Hampshire Domesday', in (156), I, 399–447.
895 —— 'Introduction to the Herefordshire Domesday', in (177), I, 263–308.
896 —— 'Introduction to the Hertfordshire Domesday', in (178), I, 263–99.
897 —— 'Introduction to the Northamptonshire Domesday', in (141), I, 257–300.
898 —— 'Introduction to the Somerset Domesday', in (190), I, 383–433.
899 —— 'Introduction to the Surrey Domesday', in (165), I, 265–94.
900 —— 'Introduction to the Warwickshire Domesday', in (194), I, 269–98.
901 —— 'Introduction to the Worcestershire Domesday', in (206), I, 235–81.
902 —— 'The Leicestershire survey', in *FE*, pp. 160–74. See (413).
903 —— 'The Lindsey survey', in *FE*, pp. 149–59. See (413).
904 —— 'The Northamptonshire geld roll', in *FE*, pp. 124–30. See (413).
905 —— 'The Northamptonshire survey', in *FE*, pp. 175–81. See (413).
906 —— 'The "virgata" ', *EHR*, 2 (Apr. 1887), 329–32. Comments on Seebohm (1095).
907 —— 'The Worcestershire survey', in *FE*, pp. 140–8. See (413).
908 Round, J. Horace and Louis F. Salzman. 'Introduction to the Sussex Domesday', in (193), I, 351–86.
909 Russell, Josiah C. 'The clerical population of medieval England', *Trad.*, 2 (1944), 177–212.
910 —— 'Mediaeval Midland and northern migration to London, 1100–1365', *Spec.*, 34 (Oct. 1959), 641–5. Review of Ekwall (761).
911 —— 'A quantitative approach to medieval population change', *Journal of Economic History*, 24 (Mar. 1964), 1–21.
912 Salter, Herbert E. 'An Oxford mural mansion', in Edwards *et al.* (eds.), *Essays . . . Tait* [see (346)], pp. 299–303. On tenures with obligations to repair town walls.
913 Salzman, Louis F. 'The Domesday survey for Cornwall: introduction', in (170), pt. 8, pp. 45–60.
914 —— 'Introduction to the Cambridgeshire Domesday', in (200), I, 335–57.
915 Sawyer, Peter H. 'The "original returns" and Domesday Book', *EHR*, 70 (Apr. 1955), 177–97. Argues for the 'feudal' nature and purposes of Domesday Book.
916 —— 'The place-names of Domesday Book', *BJRL*, 38 (Mar. 1956), 483–506.
917 Seebohm, Frederic, 'Villainage in England', *EHR*, 7 (July 1892), 444–65. Extensive critique of Vinogradoff (823).
918 Setton, Kenneth M. '900 years ago. The Norman Conquest', *National Geographic*, 130 (Aug. 1966), 206–51. A popular, lavishly produced survey.
919 Sheehan, Michael M. 'The influence of canon law on the property rights of married women in England', *Mediaeval Studies*, 25 (1963), 109–24.
920 Slack, Walter J. 'The Shropshire ploughman of Domesday Book', *Transactions of the Shropshire Archaeological and Natural History Society*, 50 (1939), 31–5.
921 Slade, Cecil F. 'Introduction to the Staffordshire Domesday', in (191), IV, 1–36.
922 Stenton, Doris M. 'Communications', in Austin Lane Poole (ed.), *Medieval England*, I, 196–208. See (55).
923 Stenton, Frank M. 'The changing feudalism of the middle ages', *Hist.*, new ser., 19 (Mar. 1935), 289–301. A suggestive general essay, tracing changes in feudal organization from 1066 to the fifteenth century.
924 —— 'Domesday survey: introduction', in *VCH Oxford* (187), I, 373–95.
925 —— 'English families and the Norman Conquest', *TRHS*, 4th ser., 26 (1944), 1–12. On the fortunes of Anglo-Saxon families after 1066.
926 —— 'Introduction to the Derbyshire Domesday', in (171), I, 293–326.
927 —— 'Introduction to the Huntingdonshire Domesday', in (179), I, 315–36.
928 —— 'Introduction to the Leicestershire survey', in (181), I, 277–305.
929 —— 'Introduction to the Nottinghamshire Domesday', in (186), I, 207–46.
930 —— 'Introduction to the Rutland Domesday', in (188), I, 121–37.

931 —— 'Norman London', in Barraclough (ed.), *Social life in early England* [see (872)], pp. 179–207. The best introduction. Originally published as Historical Association Leaflets, nos. 93–4. 1934.

932 —— 'The Scandanavian colonies in England and Normandy', *TRHS*, 4th ser., **27** (1945), 1–12.

933 Stephenson, Carl. 'Commendation and related problems in Domesday', *EHR*, **59** (Sept. 1944), 289–310. See Dodwell (846).

934 —— 'Feudalism and its antecedents in England', *AHR*, **48** (Jan. 1943), 245–65.

935 Stevenson, William H. 'The hundreds of Domesday', *EHR*, **5** (Jan. 1890), 95–100.

936 Strayer, Joseph R. 'Feudalism in Western Europe', in Coulborn (ed.), *Feudalism in history*, pp. 15–25. See (841).

937 Strayer, Joseph R. and Rushton Coulborn, 'The idea of feudalism', in Coulborn (ed.), *Feudalism in history*, pp. 3–11. See (841).

938 Tait, James. 'Introduction to the Shropshire Domesday', in (189), I, 279–308.

939 Taylor, Charles S. 'The Norman settlement of Gloucestershire', *Transactions of the Bristol and Gloucestershire Archaeological Association*, **40** (1917), 57–88.

940 Taylor, Isaac. 'Wapentakes and hundreds', in Patrick Dove (ed.), *Domesday studies*, 1888–91, 2 vols., I, 67–76.

941 Thorne, Samuel E. 'English feudalism and estates in land', *Cambridge Law Journal* (1959), 193–209. A fundamental work for the growth of hereditability and primogeniture.

942 Thrupp, Sylvia L. 'The gilds', in *CEH*, III, 230–80. See (873).

943 Wagner, Anthony R. 'Heraldry', in Austin Lane Poole (ed.), *Medieval England*, I, 338–81. See (55).

944 Williams, D. Trevor. 'Linguistic divides in South Wales', *Archaeologia Cambrensis*, **90** (Dec. 1935), 239–66.

945 Wilson, James. 'Introduction to the Cumberland Domesday, early pipe rolls, and Testa de Nevill', in (207), I, 295–335. Attempts to read back from largely later evidence.

946 Wilson, Richard M. 'English and French in England, 1100–1300', *Hist.*, new ser., **28** (Mar. 1943), 37–60. The comparative use of the two languages in the twelfth and thirteenth centuries.

VIII ECONOMIC HISTORY

1 Printed Sources

(See also sec. VII, pt. 1, above and secs. IX and XII, pt. 1, below)

947 Ballard, Adolphus (ed.). *British borough charters 1042–1216*. Cambridge, 1913. The authoritative collection.

948 Bateson, Mary (ed.). *Borough customs* (Selden Society, XVIII, XXI). 1904–6, 2 vols.

949 —— *Records of the borough of Leicester, 1103–1327*. 1899.

950 Brooke, George C. *A catalogue of English coins in the British Museum: the Norman kings*. 1916, 2 vols.

951 Hall, Hubert and Frieda J. Nicholas (eds.). *Select tracts and table books relating to English weights and measures, 1100–1742*, in *Camden Miscellany*, **15** (Camden Society, 3rd ser., XLI). 1929.

952 Hudson, William and John C. Tingey (eds.). *Catalogue of the records of the city of Norwich*. Norwich, 1898.

953 Maitland, Frederic W. and Mary Bateson (eds.). *Charters of the borough of Cambridge*. Cambridge, 1901.

954 Palmer, William M. (ed.). *Cambridge borough documents*. Cambridge, 1931.

2 Surveys

955 Ashley, William J. *Introduction to English economic history and theory: the middle ages.* 3rd ed., 1894.
956 Beveridge, William H. *et al. Prices and wages in England from the twelfth to the nineteenth century,* vol. I. 1939.
957 Clapham, John. *Concise economic history of Britain from the earliest times to 1750.* 1949.
958 Cunningham, William. *The growth of English industry and commerce.* Cambridge, 1896–1903, 2 vols.
959 Dietz, Frederick C. *Economic history of England.* New York, 1942.
960 Gibbins, Henry de B. *Industry in England: historical outlines.* 10th ed., 1920.
961 Heaton, Herbert. *Economic history of Europe.* Revised ed., New York, 1948. Useful general textbook.
962 Lipson, Ephraim. *Economic history of England,* I, *The middle ages.* 11th ed., 1956. Still the only large-scale medieval survey, but progressively less satisfactory.
963 Meredith, Hugh O. *Outlines of the economic history of England.* 5th ed., 1949.
964 Salzman, Louis F. *English industries of the middle ages.* 2nd ed., Oxford, 1923.
965 —— *English trade in the middle ages.* Oxford, 1931.

3 Monographs

966 Andrew, Walter J. *A numismatic history of the reign of Henry I.* 1901.
967 Ballard, Adolphus. *The Domesday boroughs.* Oxford, 1904.
968 Beresford, Maurice W. *New towns of the middle ages.* 1967. Very important for the growth of urbanization.
969 Brooke, George C. *English coins.* 3rd ed., 1950.
970 Craig, John H. M. *The mint: a history of the London mint from A.D. 287 to 1948.* Cambridge, 1953.
971 Darby, H. Clifford. *The Domesday geography of eastern England.* 2nd ed., Cambridge, 1957. The first vol. in Darby's monumental series devoted to the economic geography of Domesday England.
972 Darby, H. Clifford and R. Welldon Finn (eds.). *The Domesday geography of south-west England.* Cambridge, 1967.
973 Dolley, R. H. Michael. *The Norman Conquest and the English coinage.* 1966.
974 Gough, John W. *The mines of Mendip.* 2nd ed., Newton Abbot, 1967. A valuable contribution to the history of mining.
975 Gross, Charles. *The gild merchant.* Oxford, 1890, 2 vols. Still a standard authority.
976 Hall, Hubert. *A history of the customs-revenue in England.* 1885, 2 vols.
977 Hamilton, Henry. *The English brass and copper industries to 1800.* 1926.
978 Haskins, Charles. *The ancient trade guilds and companies of Salisbury.* Salisbury, 1912.
979 Heaton, Herbert. *The Yorkshire woollen and worsted industries* . . . 2nd ed., Oxford, 1965. The basic work on the subject.
980 Lewis, George R. *The stannaries.* Cambridge, Mass., 1906. Excellent and thorough study of English tin mining.
981 Lipson, Ephraim. *History of the woollen and worsted industries.* 3rd ed., 1950. Very useful general work.
982 Maitland, Frederic W. *Township and borough.* Cambridge, 1898. One of Maitland's great works, stressing the close relations between early urban communities and agrarian society.
983 Nef, John U. *The rise of the British coal industry.* 1932, 2 vols. Standard detailed account.
984 Oman, Charles. *The coinage of England.* Oxford, 1931.
985 Page, William. *London, its early origin and development.* 1923.
986 Power, Eileen. *The wool trade in medieval English history.* 1941. Almost

completely devoted to the fourteenth and fifteenth centuries, but with insights valuable for earlier periods.

987 Ramsey, James H. *Revenues of the kings of England*. Oxford, 1925, 2 vols. Useful for certain statistical purposes.

988 Salzman, Louis F. *Building in England down to 1540*. 3rd ed., Oxford, 1967. Basically a useful collection of sources.

989 Schubert, Hans (= John) R. *History of the British iron and steel industry*. 1957. From Roman times to the late eighteenth century.

990 Stephenson, Carl. *Borough and town*. Cambridge, Mass., 1933. Argues that urbanization only fully developed after 1066; for convincing criticism, see Tait (991).

991 Tait, James. *The medieval English borough*. Manchester, 1936. The great work on the early growth of English towns, showing their importance under the Anglo-Saxons; cf. Stephenson (990).

992 —— *Medieval Manchester and the beginnings of Lancashire*. Manchester, 1904. An excellent urban study, still a model of its kind.

993 Unwin, George. *The gilds and companies of London*. 3rd ed., 1938. The comprehensive authority.

994 Webb, Philip C. *A short account of danegeld*. 1756.

4 Articles

995 Andrew, Walter J. 'The die for Stephen's coinage in the Guildhall Museum', *British Numismatic Journal*, **22** (Jan. 1937), 29–34.

996 Atkin, C. W. 'Herefordshire', in H. Clifford Darby and Ian B. Terrett (eds.), *The Domesday geography of Midland England*, Cambridge, 1954, pp. 57–112.

997 Baker, John N. L. 'Medieval trade routes', in Barraclough (ed.), *Social life in early England* [see (872)], pp. 224–46. Orginally published as Historical Association Pamphlet, no. III. 1938.

998 Ballard, Adolphus. 'The burgesses of Domesday', *EHR*, **21** (Oct. 1906), 699–709.

999 —— 'The law of Breteuil', *EHR*, **30** (Oct. 1915), 646–58.

1000 Burton, Frank E. 'The coins of Henry I of the Nottingham mint', *Transactions of the Thoroton Society*, **45** (1942), 1–4.

1001 —— 'The coins of William the Conqueror, 1066–1087, of the Nottingham mint', *Transactions of the Thoroton Society*, **42** (1939), 15–18.

1002 Campbell, Eila M. J. 'Bedfordshire', in H. Clifford Darby and Eila M. J. Campbell (eds.), *The Domesday geography of south-east England*, Cambridge, 1962, pp. 1–47.

1003 —— 'Berkshire', in Darby and Campbell (eds.), *DGSEE*, pp. 239–86. See (1002).

1004 —— 'Buckinghamshire', in Darby and Campbell (eds.), *DGSEE*, pp. 138–85. See (1002).

1005 —— 'Hertfordshire', in Darby and Campbell (eds.), *DGSEE*, pp. 48–96. See (1002).

1006 —— 'Kent', in Darby and Campbell (eds.), *DGSEE*, pp. 483–562. See (1002).

1007 —— 'Middlesex', in Darby and Campbell (eds.), *DGSEE*, pp. 97–137. See (1002).

1008 Carus-Wilson, Eleanora M. 'The English cloth industry in the late twelfth and early thirteenth centuries', *EcHR*, 1st ser., **14** (Sept. 1944), 32–50.

1009 —— 'Towns and trade', in Austin Lane Poole (ed.), *Medieval England* [see (55)], I, 209–63. Valuable general survey.

1010 —— 'The woollen industry', in Michael M. Postan and Edwin E. Rich (eds.), *The Cambridge economic history of Europe*, II, *Trade and industry in the middle ages*, Cambridge, 1952, pp. 355–429.

1011 Darby, H. Clifford. 'The economic geography of England, AD 1000–1250', in H. Clifford Darby (ed.), *An historical geography of England before AD 1800*, Cambridge, 1936, pp. 165–229.

1012 ——— 'Gloucestershire', in Darby and Terrett (eds.), *DGME*, pp. 1–56. See (996).

1013 ——— 'The midland counties', in Darby and Terrett (eds.), *DGME*, pp. 417–46. See (996).

1014 ——— 'The northern counties', in H. Clifford Darby and Ian S. Maxwell (eds.), *The Domesday geography of northern England*, Cambridge, 1962, pp. 419–54.

1015 ——— 'The south-eastern counties', in Darby and Campbell (eds.), *DGSEE*, pp. 563–610. See (1002).

1016 Darby, H. Clifford *et al.* 'Social and economic history', in *VCH Cambridge* (200), II, 48–140.

1017 de Roover, Raymond. 'The organization of trade', in *CEH*, III, 42–118. See (873).

1018 Dolley, R. H. Michael. 'Coinage', in Austin Lane Poole (ed.), *Medieval England*, I, 264–99. See (55).

1019 Finn, R. Welldon. 'Hampshire', in Darby and Campbell (eds.), *DGSEE*, pp. 287–363. See (1002).

1020 Fryde, Edward B. and Michael M. Fryde. 'Public credit: England', in *CEH*, III, 451–71. See (873).

1021 Harvey, S. 'Royal revenue and Domesday terminology', *EcHR*, 2nd ser., **20** (Aug. 1967), 221–8.

1022 Hibbert, Arthur. 'The economic policies of towns', in *CEH*, III, 157–229. See (873).

1023 Holly, D. 'Derbyshire', in Darby and Maxwell (eds.), *DGNE*, pp. 278–329. See (1014).

1024 ——— 'The Domesday geography of Leicestershire', *Transactions of the Leicestershire Archaeological Society*, **20** (1938), 167–202.

1025 ——— 'Leicestershire', in Darby and Terrett (eds.), *DGME*, pp. 309–54. See (996).

1026 Jope, Edward M. and Ian B. Terrett. 'Oxfordshire', in Darby and Campbell (eds.), *DGSEE*, pp. 186–238. See (1002).

1027 King, S. H. 'Sussex', in Darby and Campbell (eds.), *DGSEE*, pp. 407–82. See (1002).

1028 Kinvig, Robert H. 'Warwickshire', in Darby and Terrett (eds.), *DGME*, pp. 270–308. See (996).

1029 Lloyd, C. W. 'Surrey', in Darby and Campbell (eds.), *DGSEE*, pp. 364–406. See (1002).

1030 Lopez, Robert. 'The trade of medieval Europe: the south', in *CEH*, II [see (1010)], 257–354. A brilliant essay, indispensable for seeing English commercial development in its larger context.

1031 McCusker, John J., Jr. 'The wine prise and medieval mercantile shipping', *Spec.*, **41** (Apr. 1966), 279–96.

1032 Maxwell, Ian S. 'Yorkshire: East Riding', in Darby and Maxwell (eds.), *DGNE*, pp. 164–232. See (1014).

1033 ——— 'Yorkshire: North Riding', in Darby and Maxwell (eds.), *DGNE*, pp. 85–163. See (1014).

1034 ——— 'Yorkshire: West Riding', in Darby and Maxwell (eds.), *DGNE*, pp. 1–84. See (1014).

1035 ——— 'The Yorkshire folios', in Darby and Maxwell (eds.), *DGNE* [see (1014)], pp. 456–94. Definitive identification of vill names.

1036 Miller, Edward. 'The economic policies of governments: France and England', in *CEH*, III [see (873)], 290–339. A most valuable comparative study.

1037 Monkhouse, Francis J. 'Worcestershire', in Darby and Terrett (eds.), *DGME*, pp. 215–69. See (996).

1038 Murray, Katherine M. E. 'Shipping', in Austin Lane Poole (ed.), *Medieval England*, I, 168–95. See (55).

1039 Nef, John U. 'Mining and metallurgy in medieval civilisation', in *CEH*, II, 430–93. See (1010).

1040 Postan, Michael M. 'The trade of medieval Europe: the north', in *CEH*,

II [see (1010)], 119–256. Probably the best introduction to the entire problem of northern European economic development in the middle ages.

1041 —— 'The rise of a money economy', *EcHR*, 1st ser., **14** (Sept. 1944), 123–34.

1042 Redford, Arthur. 'The emergence of Manchester', *Hist.*, new ser., **24** (June 1939), 32–49.

1043 Round, J. Horace. 'Danegeld and the finance of Domesday', in Dove (ed.), *Domesday studies*, I, 77–142. See (940).

1044 Saunders, V. A. 'Shropshire', in Darby and Terrett (eds.), *DGME*, pp. 113–59. See (996).

1045 Sawyer, Peter H. 'The wealth of England in the eleventh century', *TRHS*, 5th ser., **15** (1965), 145–64. An important study, arguing that England was wealthier than previously suspected, and that much of the wealth lay in wool.

1046 Smith, Arthur L. 'Trade and industry', in Traill and Mann (eds.), *Social England*, I, 512–25. See (393).

1047 Spufford, P. 'Coinage and currency', in *CEH*, III, 576–602. See (873).

1048 Stenton, Frank M. 'The road system of medieval England', *EcHR*, 1st ser., **7** (Nov. 1936), 1–21.

1049 Stephenson, Carl. 'The aids of the English boroughs', *EHR*, **34** (Oct. 1919), 457–75.

1050 —— 'The French commune and the English borough', *AHR*, **37** (April 1932), 451–67. Incorporated in (990).

1051 —— 'The origins of English towns', *AHR*, **32** (Oct. 1926), 10–21. Incorporated in (990).

1052 Sturler, Jean V. 'Le port de Londres au XIIe siècle', *Revue de l'Université de Bruxelles*, no. 1 (Oct.–Nov., 1936), 61–77.

1053 Tait, James. 'The firma burgi and the commune in England, 1066–1191', *EHR*, **42** (July 1927), 321–60.

1054 Terrett, Ian B. 'Cheshire', in Darby and Maxwell (eds.), *DGNE*, pp. 330–91. See (1014).

1055 —— 'Lancashire', in Darby and Maxwell (eds.), *DGNE*, pp. 392–418. See (1014).

1056 —— 'Northamptonshire', in Darby and Terrett (eds.), *DGME*, pp. 379–416. See (996).

1057 —— 'Nottinghamshire', in Darby and Maxwell (eds.), *DGNE*, pp. 233–77. See (1014).

1058 —— 'Rutland', in Darby and Terrett (eds.), *DGME*, pp. 355–78. See (996).

1059 Van Werveke, Hans. 'The rise of the towns', in *CEH*, III, 3–41. See (873).

1060 Verlinden, O. 'Markets and fairs', in *CEH*, III, 119–56. See (873).

1061 Wheatley, P. 'Staffordshire', in Darby and Terrett (eds.), *DGME*, pp. 160–214. See (996).

IX AGRICULTURAL HISTORY

1 Printed Sources

(See also secs. VII, VIII, pt. 1, above and sec. XII, pt. 1, below)

1062 Baring, Francis H. *Domesday tables for the counties of Surrey, Berkshire, Middlesex, Hertford, Buckingham and Bedford and the New Forest.* 1909. Useful statistical compilations.

1063 Foster, Charles W. and Thomas Longley (eds.). *The Lincolnshire Domesday and the Lindsey survey* (Lincoln Record Society, XIX). Horncastle, 1924.

1064 Fraser, Henry M. (ed.). *The Staffordshire Domesday.* Stone, 1936.

1065 Hamilton, Nicholas E. S. A. (ed.). *Inquisitio Comitatus Cantabrigiensis.* 1876.

1066 Inman, Alfred H. *Domesday and feudal statistics.* 1900.

1067 Lees, Beatrice A. (ed.). *Records of the Templars in the twelfth century* (British

Academy, Records of the Social and Economic History of England and Wales, no. 9). 1935.

1068 Record Commission. *Liber censualis vocatus Domesday-Book,* ed. Abraham Farley. 1783, 2 vols.

1069 —— *Libri censualis vocati Domesday-Book additamenta,* ed. Henry Ellis. 1816. Texts of the Exon Domesday, the *Inquisitio Eliensis,* and the Winchester and Boldon Book surveys.

1070 —— *Libri censualis vocati Domesday-Book indices,* ed. Henry Ellis. 1816–33, 3 vols.

1071 Sawyer, Peter H. (ed.). *Evesham A, a Domesday text* (Worcestershire Historical Society, Miscellany, 1). Worcester, 1960.

1072 Slade, Cecil F. (ed.). *The Leicestershire survey, c. A.D. 1130* (University of Leicester, Department of English Local History, Occasional Papers, No. 7). Leicester, 1956.

1073 Stevenson, William H. (ed.). 'Yorkshire surveys and other documents of the eleventh century', *EHR,* **27** (Jan. 1912), 1–25.

1074 Tait, James (ed.). *The Domesday survey of Cheshire* (Chetham Society, new ser., LXXV). Manchester, 1916.

2 Surveys

1075 Fussell, George E. *Farming technique from prehistoric to modern times.* Oxford, 1966.

1076 Gray, Howard L. *English field systems.* Cambridge, Mass., 1915.

1077 Neilson, Nellie. *Medieval agrarian economy.* New York, 1936.

1078 Orwin, Charles S. *History of English farming.* 1949.

1079 Orwin, Charles S. and Christabel S. Orwin. *The open fields.* 3rd ed., Oxford, 1967.

1080 Prothero, Roland E. [Lord Ernle]. *English farming past and present.* 6th ed., 1961.

1081 Slicher van Bath, Bernard H. *The agrarian history of Western Europe A.D. 500–1850.* 1963. The basic general account.

3 Monographs

1082 Barley, Maurice W. *The English farmhouse and cottage.* 1961.

1083 Darby, H. Clifford. *The draining of the fens.* 2nd ed., Cambridge, 1956. Excellent study of reclamation.

1084 —— *The medieval fenland.* Cambridge, 1940.

1085 Davenport, Francis G. *The economic development of a Norfolk manor, 1086–1565.* Cambridge, 1906. A basic work.

1086 Elton, Charles I. *The tenures of Kent.* 1867.

1087 Fowler, G. Herbert. *Bedfordshire in 1086.* Aspley Guise, 1922.

1088 Gaut, Robert C. *A history of Worcestershire agricultural and rural evolution.* Worcester, 1939.

1089 Hallam, Herbert E. *The new lands of Elloe* (University of Leicester, Department of English Local History, Occasional Papers, no. 6). Leicester, 1954.

1090 —— *Settlement and society.* Cambridge, 1965. Comprehensive study of the reclamation of the Lincoln fens.

1091 Kosminsky, Eugeny A. *Studies in the agrarian history of England in the thirteenth century.* Oxford, 1956. Contains numerous references to, and comparisons with, earlier periods.

1092 Neilson, Nellie. *Customary rents.* Oxford, 1910. A careful, comprehensive account.

1093 Postan, Michael M. *The famulus: the estate labourer in the XIIth and XIIIth centuries* (Economic History Review, Supplements, no. 2). 1954. Demonstrates the importance of hired workmen in manorial enterprise.

1094 Ruston, Arthur G. and Denis Witney. *Hooton Pagnell. The agricultural evolution of a Yorkshire village.* 1934.

1095 Seebohm, Frederic. *The English village community.* 4th ed., 1890. An elderly classic.
1096 Seebohm, Mabel Christie. *The evolution of the English farm.* 1927.
1097 Slicher van Bath, Bernard H. *Yield ratios 810–1820.* Wageningen, 1963. A basic work of reference.

4 Articles

1098 Aston, Trevor H. 'The English manor', *PP*, no. 10 (Nov. 1956), 6–14. Review of Kosminsky (1091).
1099 —— 'The origins of the manor in England', *TRHS*, 5th ser., 8 (1958), 59–83. An interesting and important work tracing the growth of seigneurial institutions in the Anglo-Saxon period and the first generation after the Conquest.
1100 Baker, Alan R. H. 'The Kentish iugum: its relationship to soils at Gillingham', *EHR*, 81 (Jan. 1966), 74–9.
1101 —— 'Open fields and partible inheritance on a Kent manor', *EcHR*, 2nd ser., 17 (Oct. 1964), 1–23.
1102 Baring, Francis H. 'Domesday Book and the Burton cartulary', *EHR*, 11 (Jan. 1896), 98–102. An early example of the value of the Burton survey (1273, 1403) in showing that many settlers in Derby and Stafford, mentioned in this cartulary, are not recorded in Domesday Book.
1103 —— 'The hidation of Northamptonshire in 1086', *EHR*, 17 (Jan. 1902), 76–83.
1104 —— 'The hidation of some southern counties', *EHR* 14 (Apr. 1899), 290–9.
1105 —— 'The pre-Domesday hidation of Northamptonshire', *EHR*, 17 (July 1902), 470–9.
1106 Bishop, Terence A. 'Assarting and the open fields', *EcHR*, 1st ser., 6 (Oct. 1935), 13–29.
1107 —— 'Monastic granges in Yorkshire', *EHR*, 51 (Apr. 1936), 193–214.
1108 Darby, H. Clifford. 'Domesday woodland', *EcHR*, 2nd ser., 3 (Aug. 1950), 21–43.
1109 Finberg, Herbert P. R. 'The Domesday plough-team', *EHR*, 66 (Jan. 1951), 67–71.
1110 Finn, R. Welldon. 'The assessment of Wiltshire in 1083 and 1086', *Wiltshire Magazine*, 50 (June 1944), 382–401.
1111 —— 'The teamland of the Domesday inquest', *EHR*, 83 (Jan. 1968), 95–101. Reply to Moore (1121).
1112 Hoskins, William G. 'The English landscape', in Austin Lane Poole (ed.), *Medieval England*, I, 1–36. See (55).
1113 —— 'The highland zone in Domesday Book', in William G. Hoskins, *Provincial England: essays in social and economic history*, 1964, pp. 15–52. Study of the topography of Devon.
1114 Lennard, Reginald V. 'The composition of demesne plough-teams in twelfth century England', *EHR*, 75 (Apr. 1960), 193–207.
1115 —— 'The composition of the Domesday caruca', *EHR*, 81 (Oct. 1966), 770–5.
1116 —— 'The demesnes of Glastonbury Abbey in the eleventh and twelfth centuries', *EcHR*, 2nd ser., 8 (Apr. 1956), 355–63. Critique of Postan (1128).
1117 —— 'The destruction of woodland in the eastern counties under William the Conqueror', *EcHR*, 1st ser., 15 (Sept. 1945), 36–43.
1118 —— 'Domesday plough-teams: the south-western evidence', *EHR*, 60 (May 1965), 217–33.
1119 —— 'An unidentified twelfth-century custumal of Lawshall (Suffolk)', *EHR*, 51 (Jan. 1936), 104–7.
1120 Mawer, Allen. 'The study of field-names in relation to place-names', in Edwards *et al.* (eds.), *Essays . . . Tait*, pp. 189–200. See (346).
1121 Moore, J. S. 'The Domesday teamland: a reconsideration', *TRHS*, 5th ser., 14 (1964), 109–30. See Finn (1111).

1122 —— 'The Domesday teamland in Leicestershire', *EHR*, **78** (Oct. 1963), 696–703.

1123 Morgan, Frederick W. 'Domesday woodland in southwest England', *Antiquity*, **10** (Sept. 1936), 306–24.

1124 Neilson, Nellie. 'Early English woodland and waste', *Journal of Economic History*, **2** (May 1942), 54–62.

1125 —— 'English manorial forms', *AHR*, **34** (July 1929), 725–39.

1126 Parain, Charles. 'The evolution of agricultural technique', in *CEH*, I, 126–79. See (838).

1127 Poole, Austin Lane. 'Live-stock prices in the twelfth century', *EHR*, **55** (Apr. 1940), 284–95.

1128 Postan, Michael M. 'Glastonbury estates in the twelfth century', *EcHR*, 2nd ser., **5** (Apr. 1953), 358–67. See Lennard (1116).

1129 —— 'Glastonbury estates in the twelfth century: a reply', *EcHR*, 2nd ser., **9** (Aug. 1956), 106–18. Reply to Lennard (1116).

1130 —— 'Medieval agrarian society in its prime: England', in *CEH*, I [see (838)], 549–632. The best introduction to the entire subject.

1131 —— 'The chronology of labour services', *TRHS*, 4th ser., **20** (1937), 169–93. Very important study of the fluctuations between demesne leasing and direct exploitation.

1132 Richardson, Henry G. 'The medieval plough-team', *Hist.*, new ser., **26** (Mar. 1942), 287–96.

1133 Round, J. Horace. 'The Domesday "manor" ', *EHR*, **15** (Apr. 1900), 293–302. Critical of Maitland (735) for regarding 'manor' in Domesday Book as a technical term connected with danegeld.

1134 —— 'The words solinum and solanda', *EHR*, **7** (Oct. 1892), 708–12. Not related to *sulung* in Domesday.

1135 Scott, Richenda. 'Medieval agriculture', in *VCH Wiltshire* (199), IV, 7–42.

1136 Thirsk, Joan. 'The common fields', *PP*, no. **29** (Dec. 1964), 3–25. Argues that the growth of a three-field system was neither so rapid nor widespread as often assumed; cf. Titow (1137).

1137 Titow, J. Z. 'Medieval England and the open-field system', *PP*, no. **32** (Dec. 1965), 86–102. Critical of Thirsk (1136).

X SCIENCE AND TECHNOLOGY

1 Printed Sources

1138 Bober, Harry. *Handschriften in englischen Bibliotheken*. 1953, 2 vols. Forms vol. III of Fritz Saxl and Hans Meier (eds.), *Verzeichnis astrologischer und mythologischer illustrierter Handschriften des lateinischen Mittelalters*.

1139 Kibre, Pearl. 'Further addenda and corrigenda', *Spec.*, **43** (Jan. 1968), 78–114. Additions and corrections to Thorndike and Kibre (1147).

1140 Sarton, George. *Introduction to the history of science*. Baltimore and Washington, 1927–48, 3 vols. in 5 pts. Sarton's massive and indispensable catalogue of scientific writers and writings.

1141 Singer, Dorothea Waley. 'Card handlist of British manuscripts in medieval science'. Not published, but available in reproduction at the British Museum and elsewhere; see *Spec.*, **42** (July 1967), 593.

1142 —— *Catalogue of Latin and vernacular alchemical manuscripts in Great Britain and Ireland*. Brussels, 1928–31, 3 vols.

1143 Talbot, Charles H. and Eugene A. Hammond. *Medical practitioners in medieval England: a biographical register*. 1965.

1144 Thaün, Philippe de. *Le bestiaire de Philippe de Thaün*, ed. Emmanuel Walberg. Lund, 1900. Edition of a bestiary composed *c.* 1135.

1145 —— Li Cumpoz *de Philipe de Thaün*, ed. Eduard Mall. Strassburg, 1873. A calendar of movable feasts, astronomical and astrological information, etc., composed for Henry I *c.* 1119.

1146 Thorndike, Lynn. 'Additional addenda and corrigenda', *Spec.*, **40** (Jan. 1965), 116–22. Supplementary to (1147).
1147 Thorndike, Lynn and Pearl Kibre. *A catalogue of incipits of medieval scientific writings in Latin.* 2nd ed., Cambridge, 1963.

2 Surveys

1148 Crombie, Alistair C. *From Augustine to Galileo: the history of science, 400–1650.* Cambridge, Mass., 1953. The best survey of medieval science, and favourable towards its achievements.
1149 Derry, Thomas K. and Trevor I. Williams. *A short history of technology.* Oxford, 1960. Condensation of (1151).
1150 Kranzberg, Melvin and Carroll Purser (eds.). *Technology in western civilization.* Oxford, 1967, 2 vols.
1151 Singer, Charles, E. John Holmyard, A. Rupert Hall and Trevor I. Williams. *History of technology.* Oxford, 1954–8, 5 vols.
1152 Thorndike, Lynn. *History of magic and experimental science.* New York, 1923, 2 vols.
1153 Usher, Abbott Payton. *History of mechanical inventions.* 2nd ed., Cambridge, Mass., 1954. Comprehensive account.

3 Monographs

1154 Bonser, Wilfrid. *The medical background of Anglo-Saxon England.* 1963.
1155 Christie, Grace I. *Samples and stitches.* 3rd ed., 1934. Contains references to the technical construction of the Bayeux Tapestry.
1156 Clagett, Marshall. *The science of mechanics in the middle ages.* Madison, 1959.
1157 Creighton, Charles. *A history of epidemics in Britain.* Cambridge, 1891–4, 2 vols.
1158 Crombie, Alistair C. *Robert Grosseteste and the origins of experimental science, 1100–1700.* Oxford, 1953.
1159 Haskins, Charles Homer. *Studies in the history of medieval science.* Cambridge, Mass., 1924.
1160 Hodgen, Margaret. *Change and history: a study of the dated distributions of technological innovations in England.* New York, 1952.
1161 Holmyard, E. John. *Alchemy.* Harmondsworth, 1957.
1162 Langlois, Charles V. *La connaissance de la nature et du monde au moyen âge.* Paris, 1927.
1163 McCulloch, Florence. *Medieval Latin and French bestiaries.* Chapel Hill, 1964.
1164 Mann, Max F. *Der Physiologus des Philipp von Thaün und seine Quellen.* Halle a.S., 1884.
1165 Talbot, Charles H. *Medicine in medieval England.* 1967.
1166 White, Lynn, Jr. *Medieval technology and social change.* Oxford, 1962.

4 Articles

1167 Creighton, Charles. 'Public health', in Traill and Mann (eds.), *Social England*, I, 526–32. See (393).
1168 Crombie, Alistair C. 'Science', in Austin Lane Poole (ed.), *Medieval England*, II, 571–604. See (55).
1169 Digby, George W. 'Technique and production', in Stenton (ed.), *Bayeux tapestry*, pp. 37–55. See (583).
1170 Hartung, Edward F. 'Medical education in the 12th century', *Medical Life*, **41** (1934), 20–31.
1171 Haskins, Charles Homer. 'The abacus and the king's curia', *EHR*, **27** (Jan. 1912), 101–6.
1172 —— 'Adelard of Bath', *EHR*, **26** (July 1911), 491–8.

1173 —— 'The reception of Arabic science in England', *EHR*, **30** (Jan. 1915), 56–69.
1174 Hodgen, Margaret. 'Domesday water mills', *Antiquity*, **13** (Sept. 1939), 261–79.
1175 Jones, Gwilym P. 'Building in stone in medieval western Europe', *CEH*, II, 494–518. See (1010).
1176 Krappe, Alexander H. 'The historical background of Philippe de Thaün's *Bestiaire*', *Modern Language Notes*, **59** (May 1944), 325–7.
1177 Poole, Reginald Lane. 'Learning and science', in Traill and Mann (eds.), *Social England*, I, 481–95. See (393).
1178 Sabine, Ernest. 'City cleaning in medieval London', *Spec.*, **12** (Jan. 1937), 19–43.
1179 White, Lynn, Jr. 'Eilmer of Malmesbury, an eleventh century aviator', *Technology and Culture*, **2** (Spring 1961), 97–111.

XI MILITARY AND NAVAL HISTORY

1 Printed Sources

(*See also secs. IV and VII, pt. 1, above, and sec. XII, pt. 1, below, for record evidence, and sec. V, pt. 1, above, for literary sources*)

1180 Davis, Henry W. C. and Reginald Lane Poole. 'A contemporary account of the battle of Tinchebrai', *EHR*, **24** (Oct. 1909), 728–32; **25** (Apr. 1910), 295–6.
1181 Farrer, William. *Honors and knights' fees*. 1923–5, 3 vols. A mass of genealogical material of great value in tracing the structure of knightly military service.
1182 HMSO. *Book of fees*. 1920–31, 3 vols. Detailed feodaries from the thirteenth century but indispensable for the descent of fees from earlier periods.

2 Surveys

1183 Beeler, John. *Warfare in England 1066–1189*. Ithaca, 1966. An excellent survey of the strategy and tactics of medieval warfare, marking a fundamental revision of the traditional views of Oman (1191) and others.
1184 Delbrück, Hans. *Geschichte der Kriegskunst*, III: *Das Mittelalter*. Berlin, 1907. Antiquated but still of use.
1185 Hollister, C. Warren. *The military organization of Norman England*. Oxford, 1965. A synthesis and elaboration of Hollister's views, stressing the continued importance of Anglo-Saxon fyrd service in the post-Conquest period; should be read in conjunction with (1207).
1186 Lewis, Michael. *History of the British navy*. 1957. Brief, popular account.
1187 Lot, Ferdinand. *L'art militaire et les armées au moyen âge*. Paris, 1946.
1188 Marcus, Geoffrey J. *Naval history of England*, I: *The formative centuries*. 1961. Standard work.
1189 Noyes, Arthur H. *The military obligation in medieval England*. Columbus, 1931. Superseded by Powicke (1192).
1190 Oman, Charles W. *The art of war in the middle ages*, ed. John Beeler. Ithaca, 1953. Reprint of Oman's brief essay first published 1885.
1191 —— *History of the art of war in the middle ages*. 2nd ed., 1924, 2 vols. Oman's great work, but now severely modified by Beeler (1183).
1192 Powicke, Michael. *Military obligation in medieval England*. Oxford, 1962. Detailed, comprehensive study, stressing a connection between widened obligation and a widened sense of national community.
1193 Sanders, Ivor John. *Feudal military service in England*. 1956. Important but

somewhat uneven, stressing the early development of reduced *servitia debita.*

1194 Verbruggen, Jan F. *De Krijgskunst in West-Europa in de middeleeuwen, IXe tot begin XIVe eeuw.* Brussels, 1954. With French summary.

3 Monographs

1195 Allcroft, Arthur H. *Earthwork of England.* 1908.
1196 Anderson, Romola and Roger C. Anderson. *The sailing-ship.* 1926. The basic work.
1197 Armitage, Ella S. *The early Norman castles of the British Isles.* 1912. Still a most valuable survey.
1198 Baldwin, James F. *The scutage and knight service in England.* Chicago, 1897.
1199 Barclay, Cyril N. *Battle 1066.* 1966.
1200 Blair, Claude. *European armour, circa 1066 to circa 1700.* 1958.
1201 Braun, Hugh. *The English castle.* 2nd ed., 1943.
1202 Brown, R. Allen. *English castles.* 1954. A good, popular introduction.
1203 Chew, Helena M. *English ecclesiastical tenants-in-chief and knight service.* 1932. Detailed study, indicating the spread of the popularity of scutage from ecclesiastical usage.
1204 Clark, George T. *Medieval military architecture.* 1884, 2 vols.
1205 Hartshorne, Charles H. *Feudal and military antiquities of Northumberland.* 1858.
1206 Harvey, Alfred. *The castles and walled towns of England.* 1911.
1207 Hollister, C. Warren. *Anglo-Saxon military institutions.* Oxford. 1962. The only modern comprehensive study, arguing for the excellence and diversity of Anglo-Saxon forces on the eve of the Conquest. Cf. also (1185).
1208 Laking, Guy F. *A record of European arms and armour.* 1920–2, 2 vols.
1209 Lemmon, Charles H. *The field of Hastings.* 3rd ed., St. Leonards-on-the-Sea, 1965.
1210 Mann, James. *An outline of arms and armour in England.* 1960.
1211 Oman, Charles W. *Castles.* 1926.
1212 Rodgers, William L. *Naval warfare under oars, 4th to 16th centuries. A study of strategy, tactics and ship design.* Annapolis, 1939.
1213 Schlight, John. *Monarchs and mercenaries.* (Studies in British History and Culture, I). Bridgeport, Conn., 1968.
1214 Sczaniecki, Michel. *Essai sur les fiefs-rentes.* Paris, 1946. Superseded by Lyon (617).
1215 Spatz, Wilhelm. *Die Schlacht von Hastings.* Berlin, 1896.
1216 Thompson, A. Hamilton. *Military architecture in England during the middle ages.* 1912. Still the standard account.
1217 Toy, Sidney. *The castles of Great Britain.* 1953.

4 Articles

1218 Archer, Thomas A. 'The battle of Hastings', *EHR*, **9** (Jan. 1894), 1–41. A polemic against Round (580), supporting Freeman's use of Wace in (511). But Round had the last word (1256).
1219 Armitage, Ella S. 'The alleged Norman origin of "castles" in England', *EHR*, **20** (Oct. 1905), 711–18. Critical of Round (1253).
1220 —— 'The early Norman castles of England', *EHR*, **19** (Apr. and July 1904), 209–45, 417–55. Incorporated in (1197).
1221 Beeler, John. 'Castles and strategy in Norman and early Angevin England', *Spec.*, **31** (Oct. 1956), 581–601.
1222 —— 'The composition of Anglo-Norman armies', *Spec.*, **40** (July 1965), 398–414.
1223 —— 'Towards a re-evaluation of medieval English generalship', *JBS*, **3**

(Nov. 1963), 1–10. This, (1221) and (1222), while incorporated in (1183), still retain their independent value.

1224 Brundage, James A. '*Cruce signari*: the rite for taking the cross in England', *Trad.*, **22** (1966), 289–310.

1225 Chew, Helena M. 'Scutage', *Hist.*, new ser., **14** (Oct. 1929), 236–9.

1226 Clowes, W. Laird. 'Maritime warfare and commerce', in Traill and Mann (eds.), *Social England*, I, 438–57. See (393).

1227 Ffoulkes, Charles J. 'European arms and armour', in Barraclough (ed.), *Social life in early England*, pp. 124–38. See (872).

1228 Glover, Richard. 'English warfare in 1066', *EHR*, **67** (Jan. 1952), 1–18. Interesting but tenuous argument for the existence of large-scale Anglo-Saxon cavalry forces.

1229 Haskins, Charles Homer. 'Knight service in Normandy in the eleventh century', *EHR*, **22** (Oct. 1907), 636–49.

1230 Hollings, Marjory. 'The survival of the five hide unit in the western Midlands', *EHR*, **63** (Oct. 1948), 453–87. Suggests a continuity of thegnly and knight service on the estates of the bishopric of Worcester.

1231 Hollister, C. Warren. 'The annual term of military service in medieval England', *Medievalia et Humanistica*, no. **13** (1960), 40–7. Argues for a clear and uniform 40-day period.

1232 —— 'The five hide unit and the Old English military obligation', *Spec.*, **36** (Jan. 1961), 61–74.

1233 —— 'The irony of English feudalism', *JBS*, **2** (May 1963), 1–26.

1234 —— 'The knights of Peterborough and the Anglo-Norman fyrd', *EHR*, **77** (July 1962), 417–36.

1235 —— 'The Norman Conquest and the genesis of English feudalism', *AHR*, **66** (Apr. 1961), 641–63.

1236 —— 'The significance of scutage rates in eleventh- and twelfth-century England', *EHR*, **75** (Oct. 1960), 577–88.

1237 —— '1066: the "feudal revolution" ', *AHR*, **70** (Feb. 1968), 708–23.

1238 Hollister, C. Warren and James C. Holt. 'Two comments on the problem of continuity in Anglo-Norman feudalism', *EcHR*, 2nd ser., **16** (Aug. 1963), 104–18. This, like Hollister's other articles (1232 to 1237), is concerned with the basic question of institutional continuity v. discontinuity between Anglo-Saxon and Anglo-Norman England. See also Prestwich (1250).

1239 Laporte, Jean. 'Les opérations navales en Manche et Mer du Nord pendant l'année 1066', *Annales de Normandie*, **17** (1967), 3–42.

1240 Lapsley, Gaillard T. 'Some castle officers in the twelfth century', *EHR*, **33** (July 1918), 348–59.

1241 Lemmon, Charles H. 'The campaign of 1066', in Chevallier (ed.), *Norman Conquest*, pp. 79–122. See (205).

1242 Lyon, Bryce D. 'The feudal antecedent of the indenture system', *Spec.*, **29** (July 1954), 503–11. Incorporated in (617).

1243 Magoun, Francis P. 'Norman history in the "Lay of the beach" ', *Modern Language Notes*, **57** (Jan. 1942), 11–16. Reference to the fyrd in Maine in 1073.

1244 Mann, James. 'Arms and armour', in Austin Lane Poole (ed.), *Medieval England*, I, 314–37. See (55).

1245 —— 'Arms and armour', in Stenton (ed.), *Bayeux tapestry*, pp. 56–69. See (583).

1246 Morris, William A. 'A mention of scutage in the year 1100', *EHR*, **36** (Jan. 1921), 45–6.

1247 Norgate, Kate. 'The battle of Hastings', *EHR*, **9** (Jan. 1894), 41–76. Unconvincing polemic against Round (580), in support of Archer (1218).

1248 Painter, Sidney. 'Castle-guard', *AHR*, **40** (Apr. 1935), 450–9. Clear and valuable discussion of castle-guard duty.

1249 —— 'English castles in the early middle ages', *Spec.*, **10** (July 1935), 321–32. Detailed study of the distribution and importance of castles in the twelfth century.

1250 Prestwich, John O. 'Anglo-Norman feudalism and the problem of continuity', *PP*, no. **26** (Nov. 1963), 39–57. A major review of the works of

Hollister (1207), John (732) and Powicke (1192), arguing that 'continuities' between pre-1066 and post-1066 military institutions are less important than the continuities between 1066 and 1485.

1251 —— 'War and finance in the Anglo-Norman state', *TRHS*, 5th ser., **4** (1954), 19–44. An article of the first importance, demonstrating the early and critical reliance of the Norman kings on mercenaries and other hired military manpower.

1252 Reid, Rachel R. 'Barony and thanage', *EHR*, **35** (Apr. 1920), 161–99. Elaborate but largely unconvincing effort to identify thegnly and baronial military service.

1253 Round, J. Horace. 'The castles of the Conquest', *Arch.*, **58** (1902), 313–40.

1254 —— 'The introduction of knight-service into England', *EHR*, **6** (July and Oct. 1891), 417–43, 625–45; 7 (Jan. 1892), 11–24. Round's most famous work, arguing for the innovative and revolutionary effects of knight-service from 1066. Reprinted in *FE* [see (413)], pp. 182–246. For criticism and evaluation, see most recently Hollister (1237).

1255 —— 'The knights of Peterborough', in *FE*, pp. 131–9. See (413).

1256 —— 'Mr. Freeman and the battle of Hastings', *EHR*, **9** (Apr. 1894), 209–59. A withering (and convincing) attack on the reliability of Wace (493), his use by Freeman (511), and the support given to Freeman by Archer (1218) and Norgate (1247). Reprinted in *FE*, pp. 258–305. See (413).

1257 —— 'The staff of a castle in the twelfth century', *EHR*, **35** (Jan. 1920), 90–7. Critique of Lapsley (1240).

1258 Smail, Raymond C. 'The art of war', in Austin Lane Poole (ed.), *Medieval England*, I, 128–67. See (55).

1259 Stenton, Frank M. 'The development of the castle in England and Wales', in Barraclough (ed.), *Social life in early England* [see (872)], pp. 96–123. The best general introduction to the subject. Originally published as Historical Association Pamphlet, no. 22. 1910.

1260 Tait, James. 'Knight-service in Cheshire', *EHR*, **57** (Oct. 1942), 437–59.

1261 Taylor, Alfred J. 'Military architecture', in Austin Lane Poole (ed.), *Medieval England* [see (55)], I, 98–127. An excellent general survey.

XII RELIGIOUS HISTORY

1 Printed Sources

1262 Arnold, Thomas (ed.). *Memorials of St. Edmund's Abbey* (RS, no. 96). 1890–6, 3 vols.

1263 Atkinson, John C. (ed.). *Cartularium abbathiae de Rievalle* (Surtees Society, LXXXIII). Durham, 1889. Records of the Cistercian abbey of Rievaulx, founded 1132.

1264 —— *Cartularium abbathiae de Whiteby* (Surtees Society, LXIX LXXII). Durham, 1879–81, 2 vols. Records of the Benedictine priory (later abbey), founded 1078.

1265 Atkinson, John C. and John Brownbill (eds.). *The coucher book of Furness Abbey* (Chetham Society, new ser., IX, XI, XIV, LXXVI, LXXVIII). Manchester, 1886–1919, 6 vols. Records of the Cistercian abbey founded 1123–7.

1266 Ballard, Adolphus (ed.). *An eleventh-century inquisition of St. Augustine's, Canterbury* (British Academy, Records of the Social and Economic History of England and Wales, no. 4, pt. 2) 1920. Largely concerned with Domesday returns.

1267 Bates, Edward H. (ed.). *Two cartularies of the Benedictine abbeys of Muchelney and Athelney* (Somerset Record Society, XIV). 1899. Records of the abbeys, founded tenth century.

1268 Baumgarten, Paul M. 'Papal letters relating to England 1133–1187', *EHR*, **9**

(July 1894), 531–41. Prints a letter of Innocent III concerning the vacant see of Llandaff, 1133.

1269 Birch, Walter de Gray (ed.). *Liber vitae: register and martyrology of New Minster and Hyde Abbey* (Hampshire Record Society). 1892. Records of the Benedictine abbey, moved to Hyde in 1110.

1270 Bourrienne, Valentin V. A. (ed.). *Antiquus cartularius ecclesiae Baiocensis* (Societe de l'Histoire de Normandie). Rouen, 1902–3, 2 vols. Cartulary of Bayeux, of great value for comparisons between the Norman and Anglo-Norman churches.

1271 Bradshaw, Henry and Christopher Wordsworth (eds.). *Statutes of Lincoln Cathedral.* Cambridge, 1892–7, 2 vols. in 3.

1272 Brewer, John S. and Charles Trice Martin (eds.). *Registrum Malmesburiense* (RS, no. 72). 1879–80, 2 vols. Records of Malmesbury, reorganized as a Benedictine abbey *c.* 965.

1273 Bridgeman, Charles G. O. *The Burton Abbey twelfth century surveys* (in William Salt Archaeological Society, 3rd ser., vol. for 1916). 1918. Records of the Benedictine abbey, founded 1004. Of great value for the information it contains supplementary to Domesday Book. See also Wrottesley (1403).

1274 Brown, R. Allen (ed.). 'Early charters of Sibton Abbey, Suffolk', in Barnes and Slade (eds.), *Medieval miscellany . . . Stenton* [see (430)], pp. 65–76. Charters of the Cistercian abbey, founded *c.* 1150.

1275 Brown, William (ed.). *Cartularium prioratus de Gyseburne* (Surtees Society, LXXXVI, LXXXIX). Durham, 1889–94, 2 vols. Records of the Augustinian priory, founded 1119.

1276 Bullock, John H. *et al.* (eds.). *The chartulary of Lewes Priory. The portions relating to counties other than Sussex* (Sussex Record Society, extra vol.). Lewes, 1943. See also (1372).

1277 Burton, John. *Monasticon Eboracense.* 1758–9, 2 vols.

1278 Canivez, Joseph M. (ed.). *Statuta capitulorum generalium ordinis Cisterciensis ab anno 1116 ad annum 1786* (Bibliothèque de la Revue d'Histoire Ecclésiastique, fasc. 9–14b). Louvain, 1933–41, 8 vols. The basic collection for the Cistercian order.

1279 Capes, William W. (ed.). *Charters and records of Hereford Cathedral* (Cantilupe Society). Hereford, 1908. Records from the mid-ninth to the fifteenth century.

1280 Caspar, Erich (ed.). *Registrum Papae Gregorii VII* (Monumenta Germaniae Historica, epistolae selectae in usum scholarum, Band II). 2nd ed., Berlin, 1920–3, 2 vols. The indispensable source for Gregory's revolutionary pontificate.

1281 Chaplais, Pierre (ed.). 'The original charters of Herbert and Gervase, abbots of Westminster (1121–1157)', in Barnes and Slade (eds.), *Medieval miscellany . . . Stenton*, pp. 89–110. See (430).

1282 Cheney, Christopher R. (ed.). *Harrold Priory: a twelfth century dispute* (in Bedfordshire Historical Record Society, XXXII). Bedford, 1952. On the Augustine priory, founded *c.* 1140–50 and dissolved 1180.

1283 Chibnall, Marjorie Morgan (ed.). 'Inventories of three small alien priories', *Journal of the British Archaeological Association*, 3rd ser., 4 (1940), 141–9.

1284 —— *Select documents of the English lands of the abbey of Bec* (Camden Society, 3rd ser., LXXIII). 1951. Charters and deeds, twelfth to thirteenth centuries, with thirteenth-century account rolls.

1285 Clark, Andrew (ed.). *The English register of Godstow Nunnery* (Early English Text Society, CXXIX–CXXX, CXLII). 1905–11, 3 vols. Records of the Benedictine nunnery, founded *c.* 1133.

1286 Clark, E. Kitson (ed.). *Fundacio abbathie de Kyrkestall* (in Thoresby Society, IV, *Miscellanea*). Leeds, 1895. Founding of the Cistercian abbey in 1152.

1287 Clark, John W. (ed.). *Liber memorandorum ecclesie de Bernewelle.* Cambridge, 1907. Records of the Augustinian priory, founded 1112.

1288 Clay, Charles T. (ed.). *York Minster fasti* (Yorkshire Archaeological Society, Record Series, CXXIII–CXXIV). York, 1958–9, 2 vols. Detailed lists of holders of ecclesiastical dignities, etc.

1289 Collar, Hubert (ed.). *The book of the foundation of Walden Abbey.* Colchester, 1938. The reorganization of the Benedictine priory, founded 1136, as an abbey in 1190.

1290 Craster, Herbert H. E. (ed.). 'A contemporary record of the pontificate of Ranulf Flambard', *Archaeologia Aeliana*, 4th ser., 7 (1930), 33–56. An important source for Ranulf, bishop of Durham 1099–1128.

1291 Darlington, Reginald R. (ed.). *The cartulary of Darley Abbey* (Derbyshire Archaeological and Natural History Society). Kendal, 1945, 2 vols. Records of the Augustinian abbey, founded 1137 and refounded a decade later, not *temp.* Henry II as in Dugdale (1298).

1292 Davies, J. Conway (ed.). *Episcopal acts and cognate documents relating to Welsh dioceses, 1066–1272* (Historical Society of the Church in Wales, nos. 1, 3–4). Cardiff, 1946–8, 2 vols. Calendar of documents relating to St Davids and Llandaff, with extensive introductions. Indispensable for the relations between these dioceses and Canterbury.

1293 Denholm-Young, Noel (ed.). *Cartulary of the medieval archives of Christ Church* (Oxford Historical Society, XCII). Oxford, 1931. Includes charters of Oseney abbey not printed by Salter (1369).

1294 Dickson, Marie P. (ed.). *Consuetudines Beccenses* (Corpus Consuetudinum Monasticarum, IV). Sieburg, 1967. Records of Bec, of great value for the study of Norman and Anglo-Norman monasticism.

1295 Douglas, David C. (ed.). *Feudal documents from the abbey of Bury St. Edmunds* (British Academy, Records of the Social and Economic History of England and Wales, no. 8). 1932. Eleventh- and twelfth-century documents of the greatest importance for the social and economic history both of the abbey and of Anglo-Norman England as a whole.

1296 —— *The Domesday monachorum of Christ Church, Canterbury* (Royal Historical Society). 1944. An invaluable collection in the same sense as (1295).

1297 Duckett, George F. (ed.). *Charters and records among the archives of the ancient abbey of Cluni, 1077–1534.* Lewes, 1888, 2 vols. Important collection of material relating to English Cluniac houses.

1298 Dugdale, William. *Monasticon Anglicanum*, ed. John Caley *et al.* 1817–30, 6 vols. in 8 pts. Dugdale's monumental collection of charters, annals, etc., of fundamental importance for all aspects of the medieval English church.

1299 Elmham, Thomas of. *Historia monasterii S. Augustini Cantuariensis, by Thomas of Elmham*, ed. Charles Hardwick (RS, no. 8). 1858. History of the Benedictine abbey to 1087.

1300 Evans, John G. and John Rhys (eds.). *The text of the book of Llan Dâv.* Oxford, 1893. Llandaff diocesan records.

1301 Fleming, Lindsay (ed.). *Cartulary of Boxgrove Priory* (Sussex Record Society, XLIX). Lewes, 1960. Records of the Benedictine alien priory, founded *c.* 1105.

1302 Foliot, Gilbert. *The letters and charters of Gilbert Foliot*, ed. Adrian Morey and Christopher N. L. Brooke. Cambridge, 1967. A superb edition of texts of major importance; Gilbert was bishop of Hereford 1148–63 and of London 1163–87. See also Morey and Brooke (1496).

1303 Foster, Charles W. and Kathleen Major (eds.). *The registrum antiquissimum of the cathedral church of Lincoln* (Lincoln Record Society, XXVII–). Horncastle, 1931–. In progress. Cartulary and other documents, of major importance.

1304 Fowler, G. Herbert (ed.). *Cartulary of the abbey of Old Wardon* (Bedfordshire Historical Record Society, XIII). Bedford, 1930. Records of the Cistercian abbey of Warden, founded 1135.

1305 —— *A digest of the charters preserved in the cartulary of the priory of Dunstable* (Bedfordshire Historical Record Society, X). Bedford, 1926. Records of the Augustinian priory, founded 1131–2.

1306 Fowler, Joseph T. (ed.). *Chartularium abbathiae de novo monasterio* (Surtees Society, LXVI). Durham, 1878. Records of the Cistercian abbey, founded 1137.

1307 —— *The coucher book of Selby* (Yorkshire Archaeological Society, Record Series, x, xiii). Durham, 1891–3, 2 vols. Records of the Benedictine abbey, founded *c.* 1070.

1308 —— *Memorials of the church of SS Peter and Wilfrid, Ripon* (Surtees Society, LXXIV, LXXVIII, LXXXI, CXV). Durham, 1882–1908, 4 vols.

1309 Gibbs, Marion (ed.). *Early charters of the cathedral church of St. Paul, London* (Camden Society, 3rd ser., LVIII). 1939. Important collection of twelfth- and early thirteenth-century charters.

1310 Goodman, Arthur W. (ed.). *Chartulary of Winchester Cathedral.* Winchester, 1927.

1311 Graysden, Antonia (ed.). *Customary of the Benedictine abbey of Eynsham in Oxfordshire* (Corpus Consuetudinum Monasticarum, II). Siegburg, 1963. See also Salter (1370).

1312 Guilloreau, Léon (ed.). *Cartulaire de Loders (Dorset).* Évreux, 1908. Records of the Benedictine alien priory, founded *temp.* Henry I.

1313 Haddan, Arthur W. and William Stubbs (eds.). *Councils and ecclesiastical documents relating to Great Britain and Ireland.* Oxford, 1869–78, 3 vols. The basic collection of conciliar and synodal decrees, to the late ninth century; far superior in scholarship to (1398) which still must be used for the eleventh century.

1314 Hart, William H. (ed.). *Historia et cartularium monasterii Sancti Petri Gloucestriae* (RS, no. 33). 1863–7, 3 vols. Records of the Benedictine abbey, first founded *c.* 681; of great importance.

1315 Hart, William H. and Ponsonby A. Lyons (eds.). *Cartularium monasterii de Rameseia* (RS, no. 79). 1884–94, 3 vols. Very important collection of records of the Benedictine abbey, founded *c.* 969.

1316 Hassall, William O. (ed.). *Cartulary of St. Mary Clerkenwell* (Camden Society, 3rd ser., LXXI). 1949. Records of the Augustinian priory, founded *c.* 1100.

1317 Heales, Alfred C. (ed.). *Records of Merton Priory.* 1898. Records of the Augustinian priory, founded 1114.

1318 Hearne, Thomas (ed.). *Hemingi chartularium ecclesiae Wigorniensis.* Oxford, 1723, 2 vols. Cartulary of Worcester cathedral.

1319 —— *Textus Roffensis.* Oxford, 1720. Rochester cathedral records. There is a facsimile ed. by Peter H. Sawyer, *Textus Roffensis* (Early English Manuscripts in Facsimile, VII, XI). Copenhagen, 1957–62, 2 pts.

1320 Hefele, Carl J. von and Henri Leclerq. *Histoire des conciles*, v. Paris, 1912–13, 2 pts. This vol. of the standard work on the councils is devoted to the eleventh and twelfth centuries; of indispensable value as a reference.

1321 Historical Manuscripts Commission. *Calendar of the manuscripts of the dean and chapter of Wells* (Tenth Report, 1885, Appendix 3, revised). 1907–14, 2 vols.

1322 Hollings, Marjory (ed.). *The Red Book of Worcester* (Worcestershire Historical Society, XLII). 1934–50, 1 vol. in 4 pts. Important collection of twelfth- to thirteenth-century manorial documents.

1323 Holmes, Richard (ed.). *Chartulary of St. John of Pontefract* (Yorkshire Archaeological Society, Record Series, XXV, XXX). Wakefield, 1899–1902, 2 vols. Records of the Cluniac alien priory, founded *c.* 1095–1109.

1324 Holtzmann, Walther (ed.). *Papsturkunden in England* (Abhandlungen der Gesellschaft der Wissenschaften in Göttingen, philologische-historische Klasse, neue Folge 25, dritte Folge 14–15, 33). Berlin and Göttingen, 1930–52, 3 vols. Holtzmann's monumental and invaluable collection of papal documents relating to England.

1325 Holtzmann, Walther and Eric W. Kemp (eds.). *Papal decretals relating to the diocese of Lincoln in the twelfth century* (Lincoln Record Society, XLVII). Hereford, 1954. With a valuable introduction by Kemp on the administration of canon law.

1326 Hugh the Chantor. *History of the church of York 1066–1127 by Hugh the Chantor,* ed. Charles Johnson. 1961. A valuable narrative source; text and translation.

1327 Hulton, William A. (ed.). *Documents relating to the priory of Penwortham* and other possessions in Lancashire of the abbey of Evesham (Chetham Society, old ser., XXX). Manchester, 1853.

1328 Hunt, William (ed.). *Two chartularies of the priory of St. Peter at Bath* (Somerset Record Society, VII). 1893. Records of the Benedictine abbey (later cathedral priory).

1329 Hunter, Joseph (ed.). *Ecclesiastical documents* (Camden Society, old ser., VIII). 1840. Miscellaneous records on the bishopric of Bath and Wells.

1330 Jaffé, Philipp. *Regesta pontificum Romanorum . . . ad annum . . . 1198*, ed. Gulielmus (= Wilhelm) Wattenbach et al. 2nd ed., Leipzig, 1885–8, 2 vols.

1331 Jenkins, John G. (ed.). *The cartulary of Missenden Abbey* (Buckinghamshire Record Society, II, X). Jordans, 1938–55, 2 vols. Records of the Augustinian abbey, founded 1133.

1332 Jones, W. H. Rich (ed.). *Vetus registrum Sarisberiense alias dictum registrum S. Osmundi episcopi* (RS, no. 78). 1883–4, 2 vols.

1333 Jones, W. H. Rich and William Dunn Macray (eds.). *Charters and documents illustrating the history of the cathedral, city, and diocese of Salisbury* (RS, no. 97). 1891. A miscellany, but important.

1334 Ker, Neil R. 'Hemming's cartulary: a description of the two Worcester cartularies in Cotton Tiberius A.xiii', in Hunt et al. (eds.), *Studies . . . Powicke* [see (390)], pp. 49–75. Textual criticism of Hearne's ed. (1318).

1335 Kuttner, Stephan. *Repertorium der Kanonistik*, I. Vatican City, 1937. Basic reference work for canonists writing c. 1140–1234.

1336 Lancaster, William T. (ed.). *Abstract of the Charters . . . of Bridlington Priory*. 1912. Record of the Augustinian priory, founded 1113.

1337 —— *Abstracts of the charters and other documents contained in the chartulary of the Cistercian abbey of Fountains*. Leeds, 1918, 2 vols. Records of the Cistercian abbey, founded 1132.

1338 Lancaster, William T. and W. Percy Baildon (eds.). *Coucher book of the Cistercian abbey of Kirkstall* (Thoresby Society, VIII). Leeds, 1904. Records of the Cistercian abbey, founded 1152.

1339 Lanfranc. *Lanfranci epistolae*, ed. Jacques Paul Migne, in *Patrologiae cursus completus, series Latina*, Paris, 1844–64, 221 vols., vol. CL.

1340 —— *The monastic constitutions of Lanfranc*, ed. David Knowles. 1951. Text and trans.

1341 Leach, Arthur F. (ed.). *Visitations and memorials of Southwell Minster* (Camden Society, new ser., XLVIII). 1891. Includes an 1106 survey of York Minster.

1342 Legg, J. Wickham and W. H. St. John Hope (eds.). *Inventories of Christ Church Canterbury*. 1902.

1343 Le Neve, John. *Fasti ecclesiae Anglicanae*, ed. Thomas Duffus Hardy. Oxford, 1854, 3 vols. Invaluable lists of ecclesiastical officials. A new ed. is in progress, but published vols. so far only begin in 1300.

1344 Liebermann, Felix (ed.). 'Lanfranc and the antipope', *EHR*, 16 (Apr. 1901), 328–32. Letters to Lanfranc from the antipope Clement III, 1085–9.

1345 Lisieux, Arnulf of. *The letters of Arnulf of Lisieux*, ed. Frank Barlow (Camden Society, 3rd ser., LXI). 1939.

1346 Losinga, Herbert de. *Epistolae Herberti de Losinga . . .*, ed. Robert Anstruther (Caxton Society). 1846. Letters of Herbert, bishop of Norwich 1091–1119.

1347 McNeill, John T. and Helena A. Gamer (eds.). *Medieval handbooks of penance*. New York, 1938.

1348 McNultny, Joseph (ed.). *Chartulary of the Cistercian abbey of St. Mary of Sallay in Craven* (Yorkshire Archaeological Society, Record Series, LXXXVII, XC). Leeds, 1933–4, 2 vols. Records of the Cistercian abbey of Sawley, founded 1148.

1349 Malmesbury, William of. *De antiquitate Glastoniensis ecclesie*, in *Adami de Domersham historia de rebus gestis Glastoniensibus*, ed. Thomas Hearne. Oxford, 1727, 2 vols.

1350 —— *Willelmi Malmesbiriensis monachi De gestis pontificum Anglorum libri quinque*, ed. Nicholas E. S. A. Hamilton (RS, no. 52). 1870. A major narrative source.

1351 Mansi, Joannes D. (ed.). *Sacrorum conciliorum nova et amplissima collectio* ... Venice, 1757–98, 55 vols. (including additions and corrections, to 1962). The basic collection of conciliar texts.

1352 Marchegay, Paul (ed.). *Chartes anciennes du prieuré de Monmouth en Angleterre* ... Les Roches-Baritaud, 1879. Records of the Benedictine priory, founded *temp.* William I.

1353 Maxwell-Lyte, Henry C. *et al.* (eds.). *Two cartularies of the Augustinian priory of Bruton and the Cluniac priory of Montacute* (Somerset Record Society, VIII). 1894. Records of the priories, founded 1127–35 and 1102.

1354 Mayr-Harting, Henry (ed.). *Acta of the bishops of Chichester, 1075–1207* (Canterbury and York Society, CXXX). Torquay, 1964.

1355 Moore, Stuart A. (ed.). *Cartularium monasterii S. Johannis Baptiste de Colecestria* (Roxburghe Club). 1897. 2 vols. Records of the Benedictine abbey, founded 1095.

1356 Noble, William M. (ed.). 'Cartulary of the priory of St. Mary, Huntingdon', *Transactions of the Cambridgeshire and Huntingdonshire Archaeological Society*, 4 (1930), 89–280. Records of the Augustinian priory, founded *c.* 1092–1113.

1357 Oliver, George (ed.). *Monasticon dioecesis Exoniensis.* Exeter, 1846.

1358 Page, William (ed.). *Chartulary of Brinkburn Priory* (Surtees Society, XC). Durham, 1893. Records of the Augustinian priory, founded *c.* 1135.

1359 Peckham, Walter D. (ed.). *Chartulary of the high church of Chichester* (Sussex Record Society, XLVI). Lewes, 1946.

1360 Perkins, Jocelyn. *Westminster Abbey: its worship and ornaments* (Alcuin Club Collections, nos. 33–4, 38). Oxford, 1938–52, 3 vols. Useful for reference.

1361 Prescott, John E. (ed.). *Register of the priory of Wetherhal* (Cumberland and Westmorland Antiquarian and Archaeological Society, Record Series, I). 1897. Records of the Benedictine priory, founded *c.* 1106.

1362 Raine, James (ed.). *The historians of the church of York and its archbishops.* (RS, no. 71). 1879–94, 3 vols.

1363 —— *The priory of Hexham* (Surtees Society, XLIV, XLVI). Durham, 1864–5, 2 vols. Records of the Augustinian priory, founded 1113–14.

1364 Ransome, Gwenllian C. (ed.). *Chartulary of Tockwith alias Scokirk* (in Yorkshire Archaeological Society, Record Series, LXXX). Wakefield, 1931. Records of the Augustinian cell, founded *temp.* Henry I.

1365 Roper, William O. (ed.). *Materials for the history of the church of Lancaster* (Chetham Society, new ser., XXVI, XXXI, LVIII–LIX). Manchester, 1892–1906, 4 vols.

1366 Ross, Charles D. (ed.). *Cartulary of Cirencester Abbey, Gloucestershire.* 1964, 2 vols. Records of the Augustinian abbey, founded 1131.

1367 Royce, David (ed.). *Landboc sive registrum monasterii B.M. Virginis et Sancti Cenhelmi de Winchelcumba* ... Exeter, 1892–3, 2 vols. Records of the Benedictine abbey of Winchcombe, founded 972.

1368 Salisbury, John of. *The letters of John of Salisbury*, ed. W. J. Millor, Harold E. Butler and Christopher N. L. Brooke. 1955–. Vol. 1, *Early letters*, of importance for general European affairs.

1369 Salter, Herbert E. (ed.). *Cartulary of Oseney Abbey* (Oxford Historical Society, LXXXIX–XCI, XCVII–XCVIII, CI). Oxford, 1929–36, 6 vols. Records of the Augustinian priory and (from 1154) abbey, founded 1129.

1370 —— *Eynsham cartulary* (Oxford Historical Society, XLIX, LI). Oxford, 1907–8, 2 vols. Records of the Benedictine abbey founded 1005, refounded 1086.

1371 —— *The Thame cartulary* (Oxfordshire Record Society, Record Series, XXV–XXVI). Oxford, 1947–8, 2 vols. Records of the Cistercian abbey, founded 1137–40.

1372 Salzman, Louis F. (ed.). *Chartulary of the priory of St. Pancras of Lewes* (Sussex Record Society, XXXVIII, XL). Lewes, 1933–5, 2 vols. Records of the Cluniac alien priory, founded 1078–81.

1373 —— *Chartulary of the priory of St. Peter at Sele.* Cambridge, 1923. Records of the Benedictine alien priory, founded *c.* 1095.

1374 Saunders, Herbert W. (ed.). *The first register of Norwich Cathedral Priory* (Norfolk Record Society, XI). Norfolk, 1939.
1375 Savage, Henry E. (ed.). *The great register of Lichfield Cathedral* ... (William Salt Archaeological Society, 3rd ser., vol. for 1924). 1926.
1376 Simpson, W. Sparrow (ed.). *Registrum statutorum et consuetudinum* ... *Sancti Pauli Londoniensis.* 1873.
1377 Sisam, Celia and Kenneth Sisam (eds.). *The Salisbury psalter* (Early English Text Society, CCXLII). 1959.
1378 Stenton, Frank M. (ed.). *Transcripts of charters relating to the Gilbertine houses* ... (Lincoln Record Society, XVIII). Horncastle, 1922. Records of the priories of Sixhills, North Ormsby, Catley, Bullington and Alvingham, all founded c. 1148–54.
1379 Stevenson, Joseph (ed.). *Anglo-Saxon and early English psalter* (Surtees Society, XVI, XIX). 1843–7, 2 vols.
1380 —— *Liber vitae ecclesiae Dunelmensis* (Surtees Society, XIII). 1841.
1381 Stevenson, William H. (ed.). 'An Old-English charter of William the Conqueror in favour of St. Martin's-le-Grand, London', *EHR*, 11 (Oct. 1896), 731–44. Prints and comments on the charter, noting its importance for the study of diplomatics.
1382 Stubbs, William (ed.). *Memorials of St. Dunstan, archbishop of Canterbury* (RS, no. 63). 1874. Collection of tenth- and twelfth-century lives.
1383 —— *Registrum sacrum Anglicanum* ... 2nd ed., Oxford, 1897. Useful lists of succession to dioceses.
1384 Tait, James (ed.). *The chartulary or register of the abbey of St. Werburgh, Chester* (Chetham Society, new ser., LXXIX, LXXXII). Manchester, 1920–3, 2 vols. Records of the Benedictine abbey, founded 1093.
1385 —— *The foundation charter of Runcorn (later Norton) Priory* (in Chetham Society, new ser., C [Miscellanies, no. 7]). Manchester, 1939. Augustinian priory, founded 1115.
1386 Tanner, Thomas. *Notitia monastica* ... , ed. James Nasmith. Cambridge, 1787. Still valuable antiquarian work of reference.
1387 Thorpe, John (ed.). *Registrum Roffense.* 1769. Valuable collection of records of Rochester cathedral.
1388 Tremlett, John D. and Noel Blakiston (eds.). *Stogursey charters* (Somerset Record Society, LXI). 1949. Records of the Benedictine alien priory, founded c. 1100.
1389 Turner, George J. and Herbert E. Salter (eds.). *The register of St. Augustine's Abbey, Canterbury, commonly called the Black Book* (British Academy, Records of the Social and Economic History of England and Wales, nos. 2–3). 1915–24, 2 vols. Largely thirteenth century and later.
1390 Walbran, John R. (ed.). *Memorials of the abbey of Fountains* (Surtees Society, XLII, XLVII). Durham, 1863–78, 2 vols. Records of the Cistercian abbey, founded 1132.
1391 Walker, David (ed.). 'Some charters relating to St. Peter's Abbey, Gloucester', in Barnes and Slade (eds.), *Medieval miscellany* ... *Stenton*, pp. 247–62. See (430).
1392 Walne, P. (ed.). 'A "double charter" of the Empress Matilda and Henry, duke of Normandy, c. 1152', *EHR*, 76 (Oct. 1961), 649–54. Attesting the foundation of a house of Austin canons at Wallingford.
1393 Warren, Frederick E. (ed.). *The Leofric missal.* Oxford, 1883. Used at Exeter in the second half of the eleventh century.
1394 Watkin, Aelred (ed.). *The great chartulary of Glastonbury* (Somerset Record Society, LIX, LXIII–LXIV). Frome, 1947–56, 3 vols. Records of the Benedictine abbey, founded 943.
1395 Watkin, Hugh R. (ed.). *History of Totnes Priory and medieval town, Devonshire.* Torquay, 1904–19, 3 vols. Includes records of the Benedictine alien priory, founded c. 1088.
1396 West, James R. (ed.). *St. Benet of Holme, 1020–1210* (Norfolk Record Society, II–III). Fakenham, 1932, 2 vols. A portion of the Hulme register, beginning with its refoundation as a Benedictine abbey.
1397 Wigram, S. Robert (ed.). *Cartulary of the monastery of St. Frideswide at*

Oxford (Oxford Historical Society, XXVIII, XXXI). Oxford, 1895–6, 2 vols. Records of the Augustinian priory, founded 1002.

1398 Wilkins, David (ed.). *Concilia Magnae Britanniae et Hiberniae* ... 1737, 4 vols. Still a standard collection, but unsatisfactory.

1399 Wilson, James (ed.). *Register of the priory of St. Bees* (Surtees Society, CXXVI). Durham, 1915. Records of the Benedictine priory, founded 1120.

1400 Woodcock, Audrey (ed.). *Cartulary of the priory of St. Gregory, Canterbury* (Camden Society, 3rd ser., LXXXVIII). 1956. Records of the hospital, founded *c.* 1087, and refounded as an Augustinian priory *c.* 1123.

1401 Wormald, Francis (ed.). *English Benedictine kalendars after 1100* (Henry Bradshaw Society, LXXVII, LXXXI). 1939–46, 2 vols.

1402 —— *English kalendars before 1100* (Henry Bradshaw Society, LXXII). 1934.

1403 Wrottesley, George (ed.). *An abstract of the contents of the Burton chartulary* (in William Salt Archaeological Society, old ser., V, pt. 1). 1884. See also Bridgeman (1273).

1404 —— *Chartulary of Ronton Priory* (in William Salt Archaeological Society, old ser., IV, pt. 2). 1883. Records of the Augustinian priory, founded 1149.

1405 —— *The Stone chartulary* (in William Salt Archaeological Society, old ser., VI, pt. 1). 1885. Records of the Augustinian priory, founded 1122–35.

2 Surveys

1406 Brooke, Zachary N. *The English church and the papacy from the Conquest to the reign of John.* Cambridge, 1931. The basic work on the subject, tracing the growth of ecclesiastical institutions and ecclesiastical–royal relations to the time of Magna Carta.

1407 Coulton, George G. *Five centuries of religion.* Cambridge, 1923–36, 3 vols. A miscellany of texts and commentaries, but still useful.

1408 Deanesly, Margaret. *A history of the mediaeval church.* 10th ed., 1959. A brief, sound introduction.

1409 Dickinson, John C. *Monastic life in England.* 1961. Good general survey.

1410 Fliche, Augustin. *La réforme grégorienne.* Louvain, 1924–37, 3 vols. The basic general work on the Gregorian age.

1411 —— *La réforme grégorienne et la réconquête chrétienne (1057–1123)* (Histoire de l'Église, 8). Paris, 1940.

1412 Fliche, Augustin, Raymonde Foreville and Jean Rousset de Pina. *Du premier concile du Latran à l'avènement d'Innocent III (1123–1198)* (Histoire de l'Église, 9). Paris, 1944–53, 2 pts. This and (1411) are basic accounts, indispensable for the wider European setting.

1413 Lawrence, C. Hugh (ed.). *The English church and the papacy in the middle ages.* New York, 1965. A series of useful general essays, including one by Charles Duggan, 'From the Conquest to the death of John', pp. 65–115, of considerable value in updating Brooke (1406).

1414 Makower, Felix. *The constitutional history and constitution of the Church of England.* 1895.

1415 Stephens, William R. W. *The English church from the Norman Conquest to the accession of Edward I (1066–1272).* 1901.

1416 Thompson, A. Hamilton. *The cathedral churches of England.* 1925.

1417 —— *English monasteries.* Cambridge, 1923.

3 Monographs

1418 Andrieu-Guitrancourt, Pierre. *Essai sur l'évolution du décanat rural en Angleterre d'après les conciles des XIIe, XIIIe, et XIVe siècles.* Paris, 1935.

1419 Aveling, James H. *The history of Roche Abbey.* 1870.

1420 Bannister, Arthur T. *The cathedral church of Hereford.* 1924.

1421 —— *History of Ewias Harold, its castle, priory and church.* Hereford, 1902.

1422 Barlow, Frank. *Durham jurisdictional peculiars.* 1950. A valuable contribution to the larger problem of ecclesiastical jurisdiction.

1423 —— *The English church 1000–1066.* 1963. An excellent study of the late Anglo-Saxon church, emphasizing its archaism.
1424 Benham, William. *Old St. Paul's Cathedral.* 1902.
1425 Bentham, James. *The history and antiquities of the conventual and cathedral church of Ely.* 2nd ed., Norwich, 1812–17, 2 vols. Probably the best of the great antiquarian compilations, especially valuable for its documents.
1426 Böhmer, Heinrich. *Die Fälschungen Erzbischof Lanfranks von Canterbury.* Leipzig, 1902. Argues for the forged nature of additions to Lanfranc's collection of Pseudo-Isidore.
1427 Burne, Richard V. H. *The monks of Chester.* 1962. Account of Werburgh abbey.
1428 Cheney, Christopher R. *English bishops' chanceries 1100–1250.* Manchester, 1950. Important study of ecclesiastical administration.
1429 Chibnall, Marjorie Morgan. *English lands of the abbey of Bec.* 1946. A valuable contribution to the entire question of ecclesiastical landlordship.
1430 Church, Charles M. *Chapters in the early history of the church of Wells.* 1894.
1431 Churchill, Irene J. *Canterbury administration.* 1933, 2 vols.
1432 Constable, Giles. *Monastic tithes from their origins to the twelfth century.* Cambridge, 1964. The definitive study.
1433 Crosby, Everett U. *The organization of the English episcopate under Henry I* (in Studies in Medieval and Renaissance History, no. 4). Lincoln, Nebr., 1967.
1434 Dickinson, John C. *The origins of the Austin canons and their introduction into England.* 1950. The basic history of the order.
1435 Dimock, Arthur. *The cathedral church of Southwell.* 1898.
1436 Du Boulay, Francis R. H. *The lordship of Canterbury.* Cambridge, 1966. Detailed, thorough study of the Canterbury estates.
1437 Dugdale, William. *The history of St. Paul's Cathedral,* ed. Henry Ellis. 3rd ed., 1818. With a large collection of documents.
1438 Duggan, Charles. *Twelfth-century decretal collections and their importance in English history.* 1963. Important for the development of canon law in England; amplifies and corrects (1406).
1439 Edwards, Kathleen. *The English secular cathedrals in the middle ages.* Manchester, 1949. The standard account; mainly fourteenth century.
1440 Finberg, Herbert P. R. *Tavistock Abbey. A study in the social and economic history of Devon.* Cambridge, 1951. Excellent contribution to the social and economic history of the church in England.
1441 Fletcher, Joseph S. *The Cistercians in Yorkshire.* 1919.
1442 Flete, John. *The history of Westminster Abbey,* ed. J. Armitage Robinson. Cambridge, 1909.
1443 Förster, Max. *Zur Geschichte des Reliquienkultus in Altengland.* Munich, 1943.
1444 Fournier, Paul and Gabriel Le Bras. *L'histoire des collections canoniques en Occident depuis les Fausses Décrétals jusqu'au Décret de Gratien.* Paris, 1931–2, 2 vols.
1445 Fox, Levi. *Leicester Abbey.* Leicester, 1938.
1446 Gleason, Sarell E. *An ecclesiastical barony of the middle ages: the bishopric of Bayeux, 1066–1204.* Cambridge, Mass., 1936. Important for the institutional development of the church in Normandy.
1447 Glunz, Hans H. *History of the vulgate in England from Alcuin to Roger Bacon.* Cambridge, 1933. The standard account.
1448 Hill, Bennett D. *English Cistercian monasteries and their patrons in the twelfth century.* Urbana, 1968.
1449 Hope, W. H. St. John. *Rochester Cathedral.* 1900.
1450 Hurry, Jamieson B. *Reading Abbey.* 1901.
1451 Knowles, David. *The English mystical tradition.* New York, 1961. Largely concerned with the great fourteenth century mystics, but of use in tracing the tradition in earlier periods.
1452 —— *Episcopal colleagues of Archbishop Thomas Becket.* Cambridge, 1951. Includes evaluations of bishops who had come into office before 1154.

1453 —— *Great historical enterprises; problems in monastic history.* 1963. Reprints of his addresses as president of the Royal Historical Society.

1454 —— *The monastic order in England, 943–1216.* 2nd ed., Cambridge, 1963. Knowles' great history of English monasticism in its apogee; an indispensable work.

1455 Knowles, David, and John K. S. St. Joseph. *Monastic sites from the air.* Cambridge, 1952.

1456 Lemarignier, Jean F. *Étude sur les privilèges d'exemption et de juridiction ecclésiastique des abbayes normandes depuis les origines jusqu'en 1140.* Paris, 1937. A basic work, valuable for its comparisons with England.

1457 Lobel, Mary D. *The ecclesiastical banleuca in England.* Oxford, 1934.

1458 Lunt, William. *Financial relations of the papacy with England to 1327.* Cambridge, Mass., 1939. The standard account.

1459 —— *Papal revenues in the middle ages.* New York, 1934, 2 vols. Valuable as a reference.

1460 Matthew, Donald J. A. *The Norman monasteries and their English possessions.* 1962. An important study, especially valuable for viewing English churches from the perspective of Normandy.

1461 Mayr-Harting, Henry. *The bishops of Chichester, 1075–1207.* Chichester, 1963. Useful biographical information.

1462 Messent, Claude J. W. *The monastic remains of Norfolk and Suffolk.* Norwich, 1934.

1463 Miller, Edward. *The abbey and bishopric of Ely.* Cambridge, 1951. A distinguished work of social and economic history.

1464 New, Chester W. *History of the alien priories in England to the confiscation of Henry V.* Madison, 1916.

1465 Oliver, George. *Lives of the bishops of Exeter.* Exeter, 1861–87, 2 vols.

1466 Oppermann, Charles J. A. *English missionaries in Sweden and Finland.* 1937.

1467 Pantin, William A. *Durham Cathedral.* 1948.

1468 Parker, Thomas W. *The Knights Templars in England.* Tuscon, 1963.

1469 Perkins, Jocelyn. *Westminster Abbey, benedictine monastery and collegiate church.* 1945. Short popular sketch.

1470 Poole, Reginald Lane. *Lectures on the history of the papal chancery down to the time of Innocent III.* Cambridge, 1915. A major work, of value for the larger context of the church in England.

1471 Raftis, J. Ambrose. *The estates of Ramsey Abbey.* Toronto, 1957. Mainly concerned with later periods, but useful as model.

1472 Raine, James (the elder). *History and antiquities of North Durham.* 1852.

1473 Rawlinson, Richard. *History and antiquities of the cathedral church of Hereford.* 1717.

1474 —— *History and antiquities of the cathedral church of Rochester.* 1717.

1475 —— *History and antiquities of the cathedral church of Salisbury.* 1719.

1476 —— *History and antiquities of Glastonbury.* 1722.

1477 Smith, Reginald A. L. *Canterbury Cathedral Priory.* Cambridge, 1943. A major study of ecclesiastical estate administration.

1478 Stenton, Frank M. *The early history of the abbey of Abingdon.* Reading, 1913. A model work of its kind.

1479 Strange, Edward F. *The cathedral church of Worcester.* 1900.

1480 Taylor, Thomas. *St. Michael's Mount.* Cambridge, 1932.

1481 Thompson, A. Hamilton. *The abbey of St. Mary of the Meadows, Leicester.* Leicester, 1949.

1482 —— *The historical growth of the English parish church.* Cambridge, 1911.

1483 Tillmann, Helene. *Die päpstlichen Legaten in England bis zur Beendigung der Legation Gualas, 1218.* Bonn, 1926. Standard account.

1484 Warburton, John and Andrew C. Ducarel. *Some account of the alien priories . . . ,* ed. John Nichols. 1786, 2 vols.

1485 Weske, Dorothy B. *Convocation of the clergy.* 1937.

1486 Whitney, James P. *Hildebrandine essays.* Cambridge, 1932. Valuable collection of papers.

1487 Willis, Browne. *History of the mitred parliamentary abbeys.* 1718–19, 2 vols.

1488 Wood-Legh, Kathleen L. *Perpetual chantries in Britain.* Cambridge, 1965.

1489   Woodruff, C. Eveleigh and William Danks. *Memorials of the cathedral and priory of Christ in Canterbury*. New York, 1912.

4 Biographies

1490   Church, Richard W. *St. Anselm*. 1870. Better treated in Rule (1500).
1491   Crowley, J. 'Gilbert of Hastings, bishop of Lisbon, 1147–1166', *Annual Report and Review of the Historical Association, Lisbon Branch*, 5 (1941), 287–313. For English contacts with Portugal.
1492   Darlington, Reginald R. 'Aethelwig, abbot of Evesham', *EHR*, 48 (Jan. and Apr. 1933), 1–22, 177–98.
1493   Graham, Rose. *St. Gilbert of Sempringham and the Gilbertines*. 1901.
1494   Knowles, David. *Saints and scholars*. Cambridge, 1962. Brief sketches, including Lanfranc, Anselm, Aelred of Rievaulx, Henry of Winchester and Gilbert Foliot. Taken from (1454).
1495   Macdonald, Allan J. *Lanfranc*. 2nd ed., 1944. The best biography.
1496   Morey, Adrian and Christopher N. L. Brooke. *Gilbert Foliot and his letters*. Cambridge, 1965. A major work, supplementary to (1302).
1497   Nicholl, Donald. *Thurstan, archbishop of York (1114–1140)*. York, 1964. A lively account.
1498   Rigg, James M. *St. Anselm of Canterbury*. 1896.
1499   Robinson, J. Armitage. *Gilbert Crispin, abbot of Westminster*. Cambridge, 1911. A fundamental work for all aspects of the Anglo-Norman church.
1500   Rule, Martin. *The life and times of St. Anselm, archbishop of Canterbury*. 1883, 2 vols.
1501   Saltman, Avrom. *Theobald archbishop of Canterbury*. 1956. The biographical information less important than the full-scale study of surviving charters, letters, etc., seen in the context of the institutional development of the archiepiscopate.
1502   Tarleton, Alfred H. *Nicholas Breakspear*. 1896. Inadequate biography of Pope Adrian IV. See also Poole (1560).
1503   Voss, Lena. *Heinrich von Blois, Bischof von Winchester, 1129–1171*. Berlin, 1932. Biography of a major ecclesiastical political figure.

5 Articles

1504   Adams, Norma. 'The judicial conflict over tithes', *EHR*, 52 (Jan. 1937), 1–22.
1505   Barlow, Frank. 'A view of Archbishop Lanfranc', *JEH*, 16 (Oct. 1965), 163–77. General evaluation, stressing shortcomings.
1506   Bell, Henry E. 'Esholt Priory', *Yorks. Arch. J.*, 33 (1939), 5–33.
1507   Bethell, Denis. 'The foundation of Fountains Abbey and the state of St. Mary's York in 1132', *JEH*, 17 (Apr. 1966), 11–27.
1508   Brooke, Christopher N. L. 'The composition of the chapter of St. Paul's, 1086–1163', *Camb. Hist. J.*, 10 (1950–2), 111–32.
1509   —— 'The deans of St. Paul's, c. 1090–1499', *BIHR*, 29 (Nov. 1956), 231–44.
1510   —— 'Gregorian reform in action: clerical marriage in England, 1050–1200', *Camb. Hist. J.*, 12 (1956), 1–21, 187–8. Important analysis of the forces aiding the reformers.
1511   Brooke, Zachary N. and Christopher N. L. Brooke. 'Hereford Cathedral dignitaries in the twelfth century', *Camb. Hist. J.*, 8 (1944–6), 1–21, 179–85.
1512   Cantor, Norman. 'The crisis of western monasticism, 1050–1130', *AHR*, 66 (Oct. 1960), 47–67. The conflict of the ideals of withdrawal and activism.
1513   Cheney, Christopher R. 'Church building in the middle ages', *BJRL*, 34 (Sept. 1951), 20–36.
1514   —— 'Legislation of the medieval English church', *EHR*, 50 (Apr. and July 1935), 193–224, 385–417.
1515   —— 'The punishment of felonious clerks', *EHR*, 51 (Apr. 1936), 215–36.

1516 Chew, Helena M. 'Mortmain in medieval London', *EHR*, **60** (Jan. 1945), 1–15.

1517 Chibnall, Marjorie Morgan. 'The abbey of Bec-Hellouin and its English priories', *Journal of the British Archaeological Association*, 3rd ser., **5** (1941), 33–61. Incorporated in (1429).

1518 —— 'Early Canterbury jurisdiction', *EHR*, 60 (Sept. 1945), 392–9.

1519 —— 'Monks and pastoral work: a problem in Anglo-Norman history', *JEH*, **18** (Oct. 1967), 165–72.

1520 Clay, Charles T. 'The early precentors and chancellors of York', *Yorks. Arch. J.*, **35** (1941), 116–38.

1521 —— 'The early treasurers of York', *Yorks. Arch. J.*, **35** (1941), 7–34.

1522 —— 'Notes on the chronology of the early deans of York', *Yorks. Arch. J.*, **34** (1940), 361–78.

1523 Cooke, Alice M. 'The settlement of the Cistercians in England', *EHR*, **8** (Oct. 1893), 625–76. A detailed study, largely of the first half of the twelfth century.

1524 Critall, Elizabeth *et al.* 'The religious houses of Wiltshire', in *VCH Wiltshire* (199), III, 150–398.

1525 Davis, Henry W. C. 'The liberties of Bury St. Edmunds', *EHR*, **24** (July 1909), 417–31. Valuable for its extensive documents.

1526 —— 'London lands and liberties of St. Paul's, 1066–1135', in Andrew G. Little and F. Maurice Powicke (eds.), *Essays in medieval history presented to Thomas Frederick Tout*, Manchester, 1925, pp. 45–59. Discussion of early property lists.

1527 Dodwell, Barbara. 'The foundation of Norwich Cathedral', *TRHS*, 5th ser., **7** (1957), 1–18. On the establishment of the new bishopric in 1091.

1528 Ellis, Dorothy M. D. and Louis F. Salzman. 'Religious houses', in *VCH Cambridge* (200), II, 197–318.

1529 Frere, Walter H. 'The early history of canons regular as illustrated by the founding of Barnwell Priory', in *Fasciculus Ioanni Willis Clark*, Cambridge, 1909, pp. 186–216.

1530 Galbraith, Vivian H. 'Monastic foundation charters of the eleventh and twelfth centuries', *Camb. Hist. J.*, **4** (1932–4), 205–22, 296–8.

1531 —— 'Notes on the career of Samson, bishop of Worcester (1096–1112)', *EHR*, **82** (Jan. 1967), 86–101.

1532 Graham, Rose. 'An essay on English monasteries', in Barraclough (ed.), *Social life in early England* [see (872)], pp. 51–95. Useful general introduction; originally published as Historical Association Pamphlet, new ed., no. 112. 1939.

1533 —— 'Ecclesiastical history', in *VCH Gloucester* (176), II, 1–52.

1534 —— 'Four alien priories of Monmouthshire', *Journal of the British Archaeological Association*, 2nd ser., **35** (1930), 102–21.

1535 —— 'The history of the alien priory of Wenlock', *Journal of the British Archaeological Association*, 3rd ser., **4** (1940), 117–40.

1536 —— 'Religious houses', in *VCH Gloucester* (176), II, 52–157.

1537 Guilloreau, Léon. 'Les possessions des abbeyes mancelles et angevines en Angleterre d'après le Domesday Book', *Revue historique et archéologique du Maine*, **60** (1906), 5–23.

1538 Harvey, Barbara F. 'Abbot Gervase de Blois and the fee-farm of Westminster Abbey', *BIHR*, **40** (Nov. 1967), 127–42.

1539 Jensen, Ole. 'The "denarius Sancti Petri" in England', *TRHS*, new ser., **19** (1905), 208–77. With valuable appendix of documents, pp. 244–77.

1540 Jones, Arthur. 'Basingwerk Abbey', in Edwards *et al.* (eds.), *Essays ... Tait*, pp. 169–78. See (346).

1541 Kissan, Bernard W. 'Lanfranc's alleged division of lands between archbishop and community', *EHR*, **54** (Apr. 1939), 285–93.

1542 Knowles, David. 'Bec and its great men', *Downside Review*, **52** (Oct. 1934), 567–85.

1543 —— 'The case of Saint William of York', *Camb. Hist. J.*, **5** (1935–7), 162–77, 212–14. See also Talbot (1573).

1544 —— 'Les relations monastiques entre la Normandie et l'Angleterre', in

Jumièges: Congrès scientifique du XIIIe centenaire, Rouen, 1955, pp. 261–7. General survey.

1545 —— 'Religious life and organization', in Austin Lane Poole (ed.), *Medieval England*, II, 382–438. See (55).

1546 Kuttner, Stephan and Eleanor Rathbone. 'Anglo-Norman canonists of the twelfth century', *Trad.*, 7 (1949–51), 279–358. Of basic importance for both institutional and intellectual contacts between English and continental churchmen.

1547 Lambrick, Gabrielle. 'Abingdon Abbey administration', *JEH*, 17 (Oct. 1966), 159–83.

1548 Lancaster, Joan C. 'The Coventry forged charters', *BIHR*, 27 (Nov. 1954), 113–39. Redates them to *c*. 1140.

1549 Le Bras, Gabriel. 'Les collections canoniques en Angleterre après la conquête', *Revue historique de droit français et étranger*, 11 (Jan. 1932), 144–53.

1550 Lobel, Mary D. 'The ecclesiastical banleuca in England', in F. Maurice Powicke (ed.), *Oxford essays in medieval history presented to Herbert Edward Salter*, Oxford, 1934, pp. 122–40.

1551 Macdonald, Allan J. 'Eadmer and the Canterbury forgeries', *Journal of Theological Studies*, 32 (Jan. 1931), 39–55. See Southern (1569).

1552 —— 'Lanfranc of Canterbury', *CQR*, 120 (July 1935), 241–56.

1553 Mason, W. A. Parker. 'The beginnings of the Cistercian order', *TRHS*, new ser., 19 (1905), 169–207.

1554 Mayr-Harting, Henry. 'Hilary, bishop of Chichester (1147–1169)', *EHR*, 78 (Apr. 1963), 209–24.

1555 Miller, Edward. 'The Ely land pleas in the reign of William I', *EHR*, 62 (Oct. 1947), 438–56.

1556 Offler, Hilary S. 'The tractate "De iniusta vexacione Willelmi episcopi primi"', *EHR*, 66 (July 1951), 321–41. Shows that the tract is not a contemporary source for the trial of William, bishop of Durham, in 1088; redates it *c*. 1112.

1557 Omont, Henri. 'Les prieurés anglais de l'abbaye de Bec', *Bulletin de la Societé des Antiquaires de Normandie*, 27 (1909), 242–57.

1558 Page, William. 'Some remarks on the churches of the Domesday survey', *Arch.*, 66 (1915), 61–102.

1559 Poole, Reginald Lane. 'The appointment and deprivation of St. William, archbishop of York', *EHR*, 45 (Apr. 1930), 273–81. See also Knowles (1543) and Talbot (1573).

1560 —— 'The early lives of Robert Pullen and Nicolas Breakspear', in Little and Powicke (eds.), *Essays . . . Tout* [see (1526)], pp. 61–70. Reprinted in *Studies in chronology and history*, pp. 287–97. See (115).

1561 Powicke, F. Maurice. 'Maurice of Rievaulx', *EHR*, 36 (Jan. 1921), 17–29.

1562 Robinson, J. Armitage. 'Lanfranc's monastic constitutions', *Journal of Theological Studies*, 10 (July 1909), 375–88.

1563 Round, J. Horace. 'An Old English charter of William the Conqueror', *EHR*, 12 (Jan. 1897), 105–7. Criticism of Stevenson (1381).

1564 Saltman, Avrom. 'John II, bishop of Rochester', *EHR*, 66 (Jan. 1951), 71–5. On the possible existence of a second Bishop John *c*. 1139, i.e. after the death of John 'I' in 1137.

1565 Scholz, Bernhard W. 'The canonization of Edward the Confessor', *Spec.*, 36 (Jan. 1961), 38–60. Discusses the unsuccessful effort at canonization in 1138.

1566 Smith, Reginald A. L. 'The early community of St. Andrew at Rochester, 604–c. 1080', *EHR*, 60 (Sept. 1945), 289–99.

1567 —— 'The financial system of Rochester Cathedral Priory', *EHR*, 56 (Oct. 1941), 586–95.

1568 —— 'The place of Gundulf in the Anglo-Norman church', *EHR*, 58 (July 1943), 257–72. Important study of the bishop of Rochester, 1077–1108.

1569 Southern, Richard W. 'The Canterbury forgeries', *EHR*, 73 (Apr. 1958), 193–226. Redates the forged Canterbury claims to primacy over York from 1702 to *c*. 1121.

1570 —— 'The English origins of the miracles of the Virgin', *Medieval and*

Renaissance Studies, **4** (1958), 176–216. An important contribution to the history of Mariology.

1571 Stenton, Frank M. 'Acta episcoporum', *Camb. Hist. J.*, **3** (1929–31), 1–14. Important for ecclesiastical jurisdiction and legislation.

1572 Tait, James. 'An alleged charter of William the Conqueror', in Davis (ed.), *Essays . . . Poole* [see (443)], pp. 151–67. On Coventry abbey before its elevation to the cathedral priory.

1573 Talbot, Charles H. 'New documents in the case of Saint William of York', *Camb. Hist. J.*, **10** (1950–2), 1–15. New texts concerning the deprivation of William in 1147. See also Knowles (1543) and Poole (1559).

1574 Templeman, Geoffrey. 'Ecclesiastical history 1087–1547', in *VCH Wiltshire* (199), III, 1–27.

1575 Thorne, Samuel E. 'Le droit canonique en Angleterre', *Revue historique de droit français et étranger*, **13** (July–Sept. 1934), 499–513.

1576 Wood-Legh, Kathleen L. 'Ecclesiastical history', in *VCH Cambridge* (200), II, 141–96.

XIII HISTORY OF THE FINE ARTS

1 Printed Sources

1577 Bodleian Library. *English Romanesque illustration*. Oxford, 1951.

1578 Dodwell, Charles R. *The great Lambeth bible*. 1959.

1579 Fowke, Frank R. *The Bayeux tapestry*. 1898. Superseded by Stenton (583).

1580 Gasquet, Francis A. and Edmund Bishop. *The Bosworth psalter*. 1908.

1581 Herbert, John A. *Illuminated manuscripts*. 1911.

1582 —— *Schools of illumination from manuscripts in the British Museum*, II. 1915.

1583 Hope, W. H. St. John. *English altars from illuminated manuscripts* (Alcuin Club Collections, I). 1899.

1584 Lehmann-Brockhaus, Otto. *Lateinische Schriftsquellen zur Kunst in England, Wales und Schottland von Jahre 901 bis zum Jahre 1307*. Munich, 1955–8, 2 vols. Basic guide to the literary sources.

1585 Maclagen, Eric. *The Bayeux tapestry*. 2nd ed., Harmondsworth, 1953.

1586 Millar, Eric G. *English illuminated manuscripts from the Xth to the XIIIth century*. Paris and Brussels, 1925.

1587 Pächt, Otto and Jonathan J. G. Alexander. *Illuminated manuscripts in the Bodleian Library, Oxford*. Oxford, 1966–. In progress.

1588 Pächt, Otto *et al. The St. Albans psalter*. 1960.

1589 Royal Commission on the Ancient and Historical Monuments and Constructions of England. *Inventories of the historical monuments . . .* 1910–. In progress.

1590 Verrier, Jean. *La broderie de Bayeux, dite tapisserie de la Reine Mathilde. Reproduction intégrale*. Paris, 1946.

1591 Warner, George F. *Illuminated manuscripts in the British Museum*. 1903.

2 Surveys

1592 Atkinson, Thomas D. *English and Welsh cathedrals*. 1912.

1593 Batsford, Harry and Charles Fry. *The cathedrals of England*. 9th ed., 1960.

1594 Boase, Thomas S. R. *English art 1100–1216* (Oxford History of English Art, 3). Oxford, 1953. The best over-all survey for the twelfth century.

1595 Bond, Francis. *The cathedrals of England and Wales*. 1912.

1596 —— *Gothic architecture in England*. 1905. A standard account; many illustrations.

1597 —— *An introduction to English church architecture*. 1913. 2 vols. With 1400 illustrations.

1598 Borenius, C. Tancred and Ernest W. Tristram. *English medieval painting.* Florence and Paris, 1927.
1599 Bumpus, Thomas F. *The cathedrals of England and Wales.* 1905, 3 vols.
1600 Clapham, Alfred W. *English Romanesque architecture.* Oxford, 1930–1, 2 vols. The standard work on the subject.
1601 —— *Romanesque architecture in England.* 1950.
1602 —— *Romanesque architecture in western Europe.* Oxford, 1936.
1603 Crossley, F. Herbert. *English church design, 1040–1540.* 1945.
1604 Ditchfield, Peter H. *The cathedrals of Great Britain.* 3rd ed., 1932.
1605 Gardner, Arthur. *Handbook of English medieval sculpture.* Cambridge, 1935.
1606 HMSO. *The history of the king's works,* I–II, *The middle ages,* by R. Allen Brown, Howard M. Colvin and Alfred J. Taylor. 1963, 2 vols.
1607 Harvey, John. *English cathedrals.* 2nd ed., 1956.
1608 —— *English cathedrals: a reader's guide.* 1951. Bibliographical information.
1609 Hughes, Anselm (ed.). *Early medieval music up to 1300* (New Oxford History of Music, 2). Oxford, 1954.
1610 Jackson, Thomas G. *Byzantine and Romanesque architecture.* 2nd ed., Cambridge, 1920, 2 vols.
1611 Kendrick, Thomas D. *Late Saxon and Viking art.* 1949. A standard work; includes a discussion of Bayeux.
1612 Lang, Paul Henry. *Music in western civilization.* New York, 1941. A monumental *tour de force.*
1613 Leroy, Alfred. *Histoire de la peinture anglaise, 800–1938, son évolution et ses maîtres.* Paris, 1939.
1614 Lethaby, William R. *Medieval art,* ed. D. Talbot Rice. 1949.
1615 Pevsner, Nikolaus. *The buildings of England.* Harmondsworth, 1951–. In progress; 33 vols. to date.
1616 Prior, Edward S. *History of Gothic art in England.* 1900.
1617 Reese, Gustave. *Music in the middle ages.* 1941. The standard work.
1618 Rice, D. Talbot. *English art 871–1100* (Oxford History of English Art, 2) Oxford, 1952. A standard over-all survey of the later Anglo-Saxon period.
1619 Rickert, Margaret. *Painting in Britain in the middle ages.* Harmondsworth. 1954.
1620 Saunders, O. Elfrida. *History of English art in the middle ages.* Oxford, 1932.
1621 Stoll, Robert. *Architecture and sculpture in early Britain: Celtic, Saxon, Norman.* New York, 1967.
1622 Stone, Lawrence. *Sculpture in Britain: the middle ages.* Harmondsworth, 1955.
1623 Webb, Geoffrey. *Architecture in England: the middle ages.* Harmondsworth, 1956.
1624 —— *Gothic architecture in England.* 1951.

3 Monographs

1625 Anderson, Mary D. *Drama and imagery in English medieval churches.* Cambridge, 1963.
1626 Anfray, Marcel. *L'architecture normande.* Paris, 1939.
1627 Anthony, Edgar W. *Romanesque frescoes.* Princeton, 1951.
1628 Arnold, Hugh. *Stained glass of the middle ages in England and France.* 2nd ed., 1939.
1629 Atkinson, Thomas D. *An architectural history of the Benedictine monastery of Saint Etheldreda at Ely.* Cambridge, 1933, 2 vols.
1630 Bell, Clive. *Twelfth-century paintings at Hardham and Clayton.* Lewes, 1947. See Baker (1677).
1631 Bond, Francis. *Dedications and patron saints of English churches.* 1914.
1632 —— *Fonts and font covers.* 1908.
1633 —— *Wood carvings in English churches.* 1910, 2 vols.
1634 Cautley, Henry M. *Norfolk churches.* Ipswich, 1939.
1635 —— *Suffolk churches.* 1937.
1636 Chamot, Mary. *English medieval enamels.* 1930.
1637 Christie, Grace I. *English medieval embroidery.* Oxford, 1938.

1638 Cook, George H. *The English collegiate church.* 1959.
1639 —— *The English medieval parish church.* 1954.
1640 —— *English monasteries in the middle ages.* 1961.
1641 Cranage, David H. S. *Cathedrals and how they were built.* Cambridge, 1948.
1642 Dawson, Charles. *The 'restorations' of the Bayeux tapestry.* 1907.
1643 Dodwell, Charles R. *The Canterbury school of illumination, 1066–1200.* Cambridge, 1954.
1644 Evans, Joan. *Cluniac art of the Romanesque period.* Cambridge, 1950.
1645 —— *The Romanesque architecture of the order of Cluny.* Cambridge, 1938.
1646 Harvey, John. *English medieval architects.* 1954.
1647 Kendrick, Albert F. *English needlework.* 1933.
1648 Keyser, Charles E. *List of Norman tympana and lintels.* 2nd ed., 1927.
1649 Le Couteur, John D. *English medieval painted glass.* 1926.
1650 Lethaby, William R. *Westminster Abbey and the king's craftsmen: a study of medieval building.* 1906.
1651 —— *Westminster Abbey re-examined.* 1925.
1652 Longhurst, Margaret H. *English ivories.* 1926.
1653 Loomis, Roger Sherman and Laura Hibbard Loomis. *Arthurian legends in medieval art.* New York, 1938.
1654 Massé, Henri J. *The abbey church of Tewkesbury.* 1900.
1655 —— *The cathedral church of Gloucester.* 1908.
1656 Oakeshott, Walter. *The artists of the Winchester bible.* 1945.
1657 —— *The sequence of English medieval art.* 1950.
1658 Prior, Edward S. *The cathedral builders in England.* 1905.
1659 Prior, Edward S. and Arthur Gardner. *An account of medieval figure sculpture in England.* Cambridge, 1912.
1660 Read, Herbert. *English stained glass.* New York, 1926.
1661 Ruprich-Robert, Victor. *L'architecture normande aux XIe et XIIe siècles en Normandie et en Angleterre.* Paris, 1884, 2 vols.
1662 Saunders, O. Elfrida. *English illumination.* Florence, 1928, 2 vols.
1663 Saxl, Fritz. *English sculptures of the twelfth century,* ed. Hanns Swarzenski. 1954.
1664 Saxl, Fritz and Rudolf Wittkower. *British art and the Mediterranean.* 1948.
1665 Thompson, A. Hamilton. *The building of York Minster.* 1927.
1666 Thompson, E. Maunde. *English illuminated manuscripts.* 1895.
1667 Thomson, William G. *A history of tapestry.* 2nd ed., 1930.
1668 Tipping, Henry A. *English houses.* New York, 1921–37, 2 vols. in 3 pts.
1669 Tristram, Ernest W. *English medieval wall painting.* 1944–50, 3 vols. Vol. I covers the twelfth century.
1670 Turner, T. Hudson. *Some account of domestic architecture in England from the Conquest to the end of the thirteenth century.* Oxford, 1851.
1671 Webb, Geoffrey. *Ely cathedral.* 1951.
1672 Wood, Margaret. *The English medieval house.* 1965.
1673 Woodforde, Christopher. *English stained and painted glass.* Oxford, 1954.
1674 Wormald, Francis. *English drawings of the tenth and eleventh centuries.* 1952.
1675 Zarnecki, Jerzy (= George). *English Romanesque sculpture 1066–1140.* 1951.
1676 —— *Later English Romanesque sculpture 1140–1210.* 1953.

4 Articles

1677 Baker, Audrey. 'Lewes Priory and the early group of wall paintings in Sussex', *Walpole Society,* **31** (1946), 1–44. Argues for an earlier date than Bell (1630).
1678 Bertrand, Simone. 'The history of the tapestry', in Stenton (ed.), *Bayeux tapestry,* pp. 88–98. See (583).
1679 Boase, Thomas S. R. 'Art', in Austin Lane Poole (ed.), *Medieval England,* II, 485–514. See (55).
1680 Bony, Jean. 'La technique normande du mur épais à l'époque romane, II: en Angleterre', *Bulletin Monumental,* **98** (1939), 171–88.
1681 —— 'Tewkesbury et Pershore', *Bulletin Monumental,* **96** (1937), 281–90, 503–4.

1682 Brown, R. Allen. 'The architecture', in Stenton (ed.), *Bayeux tapestry*, pp. 76–87. See (583).
1683 Chefneux, Hélène. 'Les fables dans la tapisserie de Bayeux', *Romania*, **60** (1934), 1–35, 153–94.
1684 Colvin, Howard M. 'Domestic architecture and town-planning', in Austin Lane Poole (ed.), *Medieval England*, I, 37–97. See (55).
1685 Daniell, F. H. Blackburne. 'A pictorial record of the Conquest', *EHR*, **7** (Oct. 1892), 705–8. On a poem of Baudri (1708) as evidence for the early composition of the Bayeux tapestry.
1686 Dickinson, John C. 'Les constructions des premiers chanoines réguliers en Angleterre', *Cahiers de civilisation médiévale*, **10** (Apr.–June 1967), 179–98.
1687 Holmes, Urban T., Jr. 'The houses of the Bayeux tapestry', *Spec.*, **34** (Apr. 1959), 179–83.
1688 Kendrick, Thomas D. 'Instances of Saxon survival in post-Conquest sculpture', *Proceedings of the Cambridge Antiquarian Society*, **39** (1940), 78–84.
1689 Lethaby, William R. 'Medieval paintings at Westminster', *Proceedings of the British Academy*, **13** (1927), 123–51.
1690 Loomis, Roger Sherman. 'The origin and date of the Bayeux tapestry', *Art Bulletin*, **6** (Jan. 1923), 3–7.
1691 Mackinney, Loren C. 'Pre-Gothic architecture', *Spec.*, **2** (Jan. 1927), 11–32.
1692 Nevinson, John L. 'Civil costume', in Austin Lane Poole (ed.), *Medieval England*, I, 300–13. See (55).
1693 —— 'The costumes', in Stenton (ed.), *Bayeux tapestry*, pp. 70–5. See (583).
1694 Rosenau, Helen. 'Cathedral designs of medieval England', *Burlington Magazine*, **66** (Mar. 1935), 128–37.
1695 Swynnerton, Charles. 'The priory of St. Leonard of Stanley, co. Gloucester', *Arch.*, **71** (1921), 199–216.
1696 Thompson, A. Hamilton. 'The English house', in Barraclough (ed.), *Social life in early England*, pp. 139–78. See (872).
1697 Tonnochy, Alec B. 'The censer in the middle ages', *Journal of the British Archaeological Association*, 3rd ser., **2** (1938), 47–62.
1698 Tselos, Dimitri. 'English manuscript illumination and the Utrecht psalter', *Art Bulletin*, **41** (June 1959), 137–49.
1699 —— 'Unique portraits of the evangelists in an English gospel-book of the twelfth century', *Art Bulletin*, **34** (Dec. 1952), 257–77.
1700 Webb, Geoffrey. 'Ecclesiastical architecture', in Austin Lane Poole (ed.), *Medieval England*, II, 439–84. See (55).
1701 Wood, Margaret. 'Norman domestic architecture', *Archaeological Journal*, **92** (July 1936), 167–242.
1702 Wormald, Francis. 'Decorated initials in English manuscripts from AD 900 to 1100', *Arch.*, **91** (1945), 107–35.
1703 —— 'The development of English illumination in the twelfth century', *Journal of the British Archaeological Association*, 3rd ser., **8** (1943), 31–49.
1704 —— 'Style and design', in Stenton (ed.), *Bayeux tapestry*, pp. 25–36. See (583).
1705 —— 'The survival of Anglo-Saxon illumination after the Norman Conquest', *Proceedings of the British Academy*, **30** (1944), 127–45.

XIV INTELLECTUAL HISTORY

1 Printed Sources

1706 Anselm. *The* De grammatico *of St. Anselm*, ed. Desmond P. Henry. South Bend, 1964. Useful for its notes.
1707 —— *S. Anselmi opera omnia*, ed. Franciscus S. Schmitt. Edinburgh, 1946–61, 6 vols. The definitive edition.

1708   Baudri de Bourgeuil. *Les œuvres poétiques de Baudri de Bourgueil*, ed. Phyllis Abrahams. Paris, 1926.
1709   Benedeit. *The Anglo-Norman 'Voyage of St. Brendan' by Benedeit*, ed. Edwin G. R. Waters, Oxford, 1928. Composed *temp.* Henry I, and useful for popular cartographical knowledge.
1710   Brown, Carlton F. *Register of Middle English religious and didactic verse.* 1916–20, 2 vols. Useful for reference.
1711   Brown, Carleton F. and Rossell Hope Robbins. *Index of Middle English verse.* New York, 1943.
1712   Canterbury, Ailnoth of. *Ortus, vita et passio Sancti Kanuti*, ed. Jacob Langebek (Scriptores Rerum Danaricum, 3). Copenhagen, 1772. An unusual example of hagiographical writing by an early twelfth century Englishman living in exile in Denmark.
1713   Clare, Osbert of. *The letters of Osbert of Clare, prior of Westminster*, ed. Edward W. Williamson. 1929. Useful for spirituality.
1714   —— 'La vie de S. Edouard le Confesseur par Osbert de Clare', ed. Marc Bloch, *Analecta Bollendiana*, **41** (1923), 5–131.
1715   Crispin, Gilbert. *Gisleberti Crispini disputatio Iudei et Christiani*, ed. Bernard Blumenkranz. Utrecht and Antwerp, 1956. Valuable in reflecting anti-Jewish attitudes at the end of the eleventh century. Also printed with other works in Robinson (1499).
1716   Daniel, Walter. *The life of Ailred of Rievaulx by Walter Daniel*, ed. F. Maurice Powicke. 1950. A sensitive character-sketch, valuable for both models of biographical composition and twelfth-century religious values. Text and trans.
1717   Durham, Lawrence of. *Dialogi Laurentii Dunelmensis monachi et prioris*, ed. James Raine (Surtees Society, LXX). Durham, 1880.
1718   Eadmer. *The life of St. Anselm of Canterbury by Eadmer*, ed. Richard W. Southern (Nelson's Medieval Texts) 1962. A major work for the study of monastic culture. Text and trans.
1719   Hoste, Anselm. *Bibliotheca Aelrediana*. The Hague, 1962. Lists of eds. and studies of Aelred of Rievaulx.
1720   Lanfranc. *Lanfranci opera omnia*, ed. John A. Giles. 1844, 2 vols. See also Knowles (1340).
1721   Malmesbury, William of. *The* Vita Wulfstani *of William of Malmesbury*, ed. Reginald R. Darlington (Camden Society, 3rd ser., XL). 1928. A work of great value for intellectual attitudes and for the political–ecclesiastical issues precipitated by the Conquest.
1722   Markyate, Christina of. *The life of Christina of Markyate*, ed. Charles H. Talbot. Oxford, 1959. The life of an early twelfth-century recluse.
1723   Monmouth, Geoffrey of. *Geoffrey of Monmouth*: Historia regum Brittaniae, ed. Jacob Hammer. Cambridge, Mass., 1951. The best ed. of a major work of twelfth-century historiography.
1724   Moore, Grace E. (ed.). *The Middle English verse life of Edward the Confessor.* Philadelphia, 1942.
1725   Raby, Frederick J. E. (ed.). *The Oxford book of medieval Latin verse.* Oxford, 1959.
1726   Rievaulx, Aelred of. *Ailred of Rievaulx*, De anima, ed. Charles H. Talbot. New York, 1952.
1727   —— *For Christ luve: prayers of Saint Aelred, abbot of Rievaulx*, ed. Anselm Hoste. The Hague, 1965.
1728   —— *Sermones inediti B. Aelredi abbatis Rievallensis*, ed. Charles H. Talbot. Rome, 1952.
1729   Salisbury, John of. *Iohannis Saresberiensis episcopi Carnotensis* Metalogicon, ed. Clement C. J. Webb. Oxford, 1929, 2 vols. An indispensable work for twelfth-century humanism and the history of education.
1730   —— *Iohannis Saresberiensis episcopi Carnotensis* Policraticus, ed. Clement C. J. Webb. Oxford, 1909, 2 vols. John's famous political treatise, composed 1159 but largely shaped by the political conditions of Stephen's reign.

1731 —— *Iohannis Saresberiensis opera omnia*, ed. John A. Giles (Patres Ecclesiae Anglicanae). Oxford, 1845, 5 vols.

1732 Vacarius. *The* Liber pauperum *of Vacarius*, ed. Francis de Zulueta (Selden Society, XLIV). 1927. Definitive text, with an excellent Introduction, of Vacarius' extracts from and glosses on the *Corpus Juris Civilis*; fundamental for the study of Roman Law in England.

2 Surveys

1733 Bolgar, Robert R. *The classical heritage and its beneficiaries*. 1954. A brilliant study of the impact of the classical tradition on medieval and Renaissance educational organization and thought.

1734 Copleston, Frederick C. *History of philosophy*, II: *Augustine to Scotus*. 1959. Includes a brief but thorough chapter on Anselm.

1735 Curtius, Ernst R. *European literature and the Latin middle ages*, trans. New York, 1953. A massive, eclectic work, tracing patterns of thought and cultural continuities to Dante.

1736 Gilson, Etienne. *History of Christian philosophy in the middle ages*. 1955. A standard account.

1737 —— *Reason and revelation in the middle ages*. New York, 1938. Anselm as a prime example of the transcendental tradition which Aquinas harmonized with Aristotelian rationalism.

1738 —— *The spirit of medieval philosophy*. New York, 1936.

1739 Grabmann, Martin. *Geschichte der katholischen Theologie*. Freiburg, 1933.

1740 Haskins, Charles Homer. *The renaissance of the twelfth century*. Cambridge (Mass.), 1927. Haskin's most famous work and still very valuable for its scope.

1741 Heer, Friedrich. *Intellectual history of Europe*, trans. Cleveland, 1966. A brilliant *tour de force*.

1742 Leclerq, Jean. *The love of learning and the desire for God*, trans. New York, 1961. Comprehensive study of monastic culture to the twelfth century.

1743 Leff, Gordon. *Medieval thought from Saint Augustine to Ockham*. Harmondsworth, 1958. A most useful introduction.

1744 Manitius, Max. *Geschichte der lateinischen Literatur des Mittelalters*. Munich, 1911–31, 3 vols. The basic account.

1745 Raby, Frederick J. E. *A history of Christian Latin poetry from the beginnings to the close of the middle ages*. 2nd ed., Oxford, 1953.

1746 —— *A history of secular Latin poetry in the middle ages*. Oxford, 1934, 2 vols.

1747 Rashdall, Hastings. *The universities of Europe in the middle ages*, ed. F. Maurice Powicke and Alfred B. Emden. Oxford, 1936, 3 vols. The basic work, useful for references to pre-university schools.

1748 Sandys, John E. *History of classical scholarship*. Cambridge, 1903–8, 3 vols.

1749 Steinen, Wolfram von den. *Der Kosmos des Mittelalters*. Bern and Munich, 1959. Impressionistic survey of medieval culture, ninth to twelfth centuries.

3 Monographs

1750 Chenu, Marie-Dominique. *La théologie au douzième siécle*. Paris, 1957. Portions trans. as *Nature, man, and society in the twelfth century*, ed. Jerome Taylor and Lester K. Little. Chicago, 1968.

1751 Colish, Marcia L. *The mirror of language: a study in the medieval theory of knowledge*. New Haven, 1968. Relations between symbolism and epistemology in major thinkers, including Anselm.

1752 Darlington, Reginald R. *Anglo-Norman historians*. 1947. General evaluation of the historiographical conventions and qualities of the chroniclers.

1753 de Ghellinck, Joseph. *Le mouvement théologique du XIIe siècle*. 2nd ed., Bruges, 1948. A basic work for the impact of Aristotle's logical writings on twelfth-century theology.

1754 Douglas, David C. *English scholars*. 2nd ed., 1951. Focuses on seventeenth-century historical scholarship and the efforts of scholars to trace continuities from early English history to their own day.

1755 —— *The Norman Conquest and British historians*. Glasgow, 1946. Traces changing historiographical attitudes towards the 'value' of the Conquest.

1756 Hanning, Robert W. *The vision of history in early Britain from Gildas to Geoffrey of Monmouth*. New York, 1966. Sees Geoffrey as breaking new historiographical grounds.

1757 Haskins, Charles Homer. *Studies in medieval culture*. Oxford, 1929. Valuable collection of articles, mostly on the twelfth century.

1758 Henry, Desmond P. *The logic of St. Anselm*. Oxford, 1967. Detailed study of Anselm's logical system.

1759 Körting, Gustav. *Wilhelm von Poitiers Gesta Guilelmi ducis Normannorum et regis Anglorum: ein Beitrag zur anglo-normannischen Historiographie*. Dresden, 1875.

1760 Koyré, Alexandre. *L'Idée de Dieu dans la philosophie de St. Anselme*. Paris, 1923.

1761 Leach, Arthur F. *The schools of medieval England*. 1915.

1762 Legge, M. Dominica. *Anglo-Norman in the cloisters*. Edinburgh, 1950. Study of Anglo-Norman religious literature.

1763 —— *Anglo-Norman literature and its background*. Oxford, 1963. Useful general work on a wide variety of texts written in Anglo-Norman.

1764 Liebeschütz, Hans. *Medieval humanism in the life and writings of John of Salisbury*. 1950. A valuable and thorough study.

1765 Misch, Georg. *Geschichte der Autobiographie*, III, *Das Mittelalter*. Frankfurt a. M., 1959–62, 2 pts. Includes Anselm, Aelred, and later English figures.

1766 Pocock, John G. A. *The ancient constitution and the feudal law*. Cambridge, 1957. Valuable study of seventeenth-century historical thinking on the medieval constitution.

1767 Richter, Heinz. *Englische Geschichtsschreiber des 12. Jahrhunderts*. Berlin, 1938.

1768 Rickard, Peter. *Britain in medieval French literature*. Cambridge, 1956. Useful for the movement of ideas.

1769 Robinson, J. Armitage. *Two Glastonbury legends*. Cambridge, 1926. The development of the Arthurian tradition. See also Treharne (1778).

1770 Schirmer, Walter F. and Ulrich Broich. *Studien zum literarischen Patronat im England des 12. Jahrhunderts*. Cologne, 1962.

1771 Smalley, Beryl. *The study of the bible in the middle ages*. 2nd ed., Oxford, 1952. A book of fundamental importance, focusing on Bible studies in northern Europe in the twelfth and thirteenth centuries.

1772 Southern, Richard W. *St. Anselm and his biographer: a study of monastic life and thought 1059–c. 1130*. Cambridge, 1963. A distinguished work, treating both Anselm and Eadmer firmly within the intellectual climate of their time.

1773 Spörl, Johannes. *Grundformen hochmittelalterlicher Geschichtsanschauung. Studien zum Weltbild der Geschichtsschreiber des 12. Jahrhunderts*. Munich, 1935.

1774 Tatlock, John S. P. *The legendary history of Britain*. Berkeley, 1950. On Geoffrey of Monmouth and Wace.

1775 Taylor, John. *Medieval historical writing in Yorkshire*. York, 1961. Analysis of northern English historians, with useful references to critical editions and manuscripts.

1776 Thompson, James W. *A history of historical writing*. New York, 1942, 2 vols. Dated but still useful for medieval historiography.

1777 —— *The medieval library*. Chicago, 1939.

1778 Treharne, Reginald F. *The Glastonbury legends*. 1967. See also Robinson (1769).

1779 Wilmart, André. *Auteurs spirituels et textes dévots du moyen âge latin*. Paris, 1932. A fundamental work for the study of medieval spirituality; contains considerable material on Anselm and Eadmer among others.

4 Biographies

1780 Bliemetzrieder, Franz J. *Adelhard von Bath.* Munich, 1935. On the translator of Greek and Arabic scientific and philosophical works. See also Haskins (1172).
1781 Courtney, Francis. *Cardinal Robert Pullen: an English theologian of the twelfth century.* Rome, 1954.
1782 Hallier, Amédée. *Un éducateur monastique: Aelred de Rievaulx.* Paris, 1959.
1783 Harvey, Thomas E. *Saint Aelred of Rievaulx.* 1932.
1784 James, Montague Rhodes. *Two ancient English scholars: St. Aldhelm and William of Malmesbury.* Glasgow, 1931.
1785 Stolz, Anselm. *Anselm von Canterbury.* Munich, 1937. Trans. of works into German, with extensive introductions.
1786 Webb, Clement C. J. *John of Salisbury.* 1932. The standard biography.

5 Articles

1787 Baudry, Léon. 'La préscience divine chez S. Anselme', *Archives d'histoire doctrinale et littéraire du moyen âge* (1942), 223–37.
1788 Bayart, Jean. 'The concept of mystery according to St. Anselm of Canterbury', *Recherches de théologie ancienne et médiévale*, 9 (Apr. 1937), 125–66.
1789 Bell, Alexander. 'Maistre Geffrai Gaimar', *Medium Aevum*, 7 (Oct. 1938), 184–98.
1790 Bliemetzrieder, Franz J. 'L'œuvre d'Anselm de Laon et la littérature théologique contemporaine', *Recherches de théologie ancienne et médiévale*, 6 (July 1934), 261–83; 7 (Jan. 1935), 28–51. Largely discusses the work of Hugh, abbot of Reading and archbishop of Rouen.
1791 —— 'Robert von Melun and die Schule Anselms von Laon', *Zeitschrift für Kirchengeschichte*, 53 (Jan. 1934), 117–70. On Master Robert, an important theologian and later (1163–7) bishop of Hereford. See also Lilley (1810).
1792 Cappuyns, Maïeul. 'L'argument de S. Anselme', *Recherches de théologie ancienne et médiévale*, 6 (July 1934), 313–30.
1793 David, Charles W. 'The claim of King Henry I to be called learned', in Charles H. Taylor and John L. LaMonte (eds.), *Anniversary essays in medieval history by students of Charles Homer Haskins*, Boston and New York, 1929, pp. 45–56.
1794 Deanesly, Margaret. 'Medieval schools to c. 1300', in *CMH*, v, 765–79. See (375).
1795 Delhaye, Philippe. 'L'enseignement de la philosophie morale au XIIe siècle', *Mediaeval Studies*, 11 (1949), 77–99.
1796 Emden, Alfred B. 'Learning and education', in Austin Lane Poole (ed.), *Medieval England*, 11, 515–40. See (55).
1797 Farmer, Hugh. 'William of Malmesbury's life and works', *JEH*, 13 (Apr. 1962), 39–54.
1798 Galbraith, Vivian H. 'The literacy of the medieval English kings', *Proceedings of the British Academy*, 21 (1935), 201–38.
1799 Graham, Rose. 'The intellectual influence of English monasteries between the tenth and twelfth centuries', *TRHS*, new ser., 17 (1903), 23–65. Useful general survey.
1800 Heningham, Eleanor K. 'The genuineness of the *Vita Aeduuardi regis*', *Spec.*, 21 (Oct. 1946), 419–56. Argues for c. 1075 as the date of composition; see also Southern (1830).
1801 Holland, Thomas E. 'The origin of the university of Oxford', *EHR*, 6 (Apr. 1891), 238–49. Gradual growth of the university from early twelfth-century schools.
1802 Jennings, J. C. 'The writings of Prior Dominic of Evesham', *EHR*, 77 (Apr. 1962), 298–304.
1803 Ker, Neil R. 'William of Malmesbury's handwriting', *EHR*, 59 (Sept. 1944), 371–6.

INTELLECTUAL HISTORY

1804 Knowles, David. 'The cultural influence of English medieval monasteries', *Camb. Hist. J.*, 7 (1943), 146–59.
1805 Landgraf, Artur. 'Studie zur Theologie des zwölften Jahrhunderts, II: Literarhistorische Bemerkungen zu den Sentenzen des Robertus Pullus', *Trad.*, 1 (1943), 210–22.
1806 Legge, M. Dominica. 'Anglo-Norman and the historian', *Hist.*, new ser., 26 (Dec. 1943), 163–75. On the use of texts in Anglo-Norman for cultural history.
1807 —— 'The French language and the English cloister', in Ruffer (ed.), *Studies . . . Graham*, pp. 146–62. See (839).
1808 —— 'La précocité de la littérature anglo-normande', *Cahiers de civilisation médiévale*, 8 (July–Dec. 1965), 327–49.
1809 Liebermann, Felix. 'Magister Vacarius', *EHR*, 11 (Apr. and July 1896), 305–14, 514–15. The career of Vacarius in England from the 1140's.
1810 Lilley, Alfred L. 'A Christological controversy of the twelfth century', *Journal of Theological Studies*, 39 (July 1938), 225–38. On Robert of Melun.
1811 Little, Andrew G. 'Theological schools in medieval England', *EHR*, 55 (Oct. 1940), 624–30.
1812 Malcolm, Norman. 'Anselm's ontological arguments', *Philosophical Review*, 69 (Jan. 1960), 41–62.
1813 Pegis, Anton C. 'St. Anselm and the argument of the "Proslogion" ', *Mediaeval Studies*, 28 (1966), 238–67. Largely concerned with what Thomas Aquinas did with it.
1814 Petry, Ray C. 'Three medieval chroniclers: monastic historiography and biblical eschatology in Hugh of St. Victor, Otto of Freising, and Orderic Vitalis', *Church History*, 34 (Sept. 1965), 282–93.
1815 Poole, Reginald Lane. 'The early correspondence of John of Salisbury', in *Studies in chronology and history*, pp. 259–86. See (115).
1816 —— 'John of Salisbury at the papal court', *EHR*, 38 (July 1923), 321–30. Reprinted in *Studies in chronology and history*, pp. 248–58. See (115).
1817 —— 'The masters of the schools at Paris and Chartres in John of Salisbury's time', *EHR*, 35 (July 1920), 321–42. Reprinted in *Studies in chronology and history*, pp. 223–47. See (115).
1818 Powicke, F. Maurice. 'Aelred of Rievaulx and his biographer Walter Daniel', *BJRL*, 6 (July 1921–Jan. 1922), 310–51, 452–521.
1819 Richardson, Henry G. 'The schools of Northampton in the twelfth century', *EHR*, 56 (Oct. 1941), 595–605.
1820 Salter, Herbert E. 'Geoffrey of Monmouth and Oxford', *EHR*, 34 (July 1919), 382–5.
1821 —— 'The medieval university of Oxford', *Hist.*, new ser., 14 (Apr. 1929), 57–61.
1822 Schmitt, Franciscus S. 'Les corrections de S. Anselme à son *Monologion*', *Revue bénédictine*, 50 (1938), 194–205.
1823 —— 'Zur Chronologie der Werke des hl. Anselm von Canterbury', *Revue bénédictine*, 44 (1932), 322–50.
1824 Scholz, Bernhard W. 'Eadmer's life of Bregwine, archbishop of Canterbury, 761–764', *Trad.*, 22 (1966), 311–45.
1825 Schutt, Marie. 'The literary form of William of Malmesbury's "Gesta regum" ', *EHR*, 46 (Apr. 1931), 255–60. Shows his reliance on Suetonius.
1826 Slover, Clark H. 'William of Malmesbury and the Irish', *Spec.*, 2 (July 1927), 268–83.
1827 Smalley, Beryl. 'Andrew of St. Victor, abbot of Wigmore: a twelfth century Hebraist', *Recherches de théologie ancienne et médiévale*, 10 (Oct. 1938), 358–73. On the leading Biblical scholar of the mid- and late twelfth century; incorporated in (1771).
1828 —— 'Gilbertus Universalis, bishop of London (1128–34) and the problem of the "Glossa Ordinaria" ', *Recherches de théologie ancienne et médiévale*, 7 (July 1935), 235–62; 8 (Jan. 1936), 24–60.
1829 —— 'La Glossa Ordinaria. Quelques prédécesseurs d'Anselme de Laon', *Recherches de théologie ancienne et médiévale*, 9 (Oct. 1937), 365–400.
1830 Southern, Richard W. 'The first "Life of Edward the Confessor" ', *EHR*,

58 (Oct. 1943), 385–400. On the dating and value of the *Vita*; see Heningham (1800).

1831 —— 'Lanfranc of Bec and Beregar of Tours', in Hunt *et al.* (eds.), *Studies . . . Powicke* [see (390)], pp. 27–48. A comparison of them as grammarians and dialecticians.

1832 —— 'The place of England in the twelfth-century renaissance', *Hist.*, new ser., **45** (Oct. 1960), 201–16. An illuminating general account, very valuable as an introduction.

1833 —— 'St. Anselm and his English pupils', *Medieval and Renaissance Studies*, **I** (1941), 3–34.

1834 Stolz, Anselm. 'Das Proslogion des heiligen Anselm', *Revue bénédictine*, **47** (1935), 331–47.

1835 Tatlock, John S. P. 'Certain contemporaneous matters in Geoffrey of Monmouth', *Spec.*, **6** (Apr. 1931), 206–24.

1836 —— 'Geoffrey of Monmouth's motives for writing his *Historia*', *Proceedings of the American Philosophical Society*, **79** (Nov. 1938), 695–703.

1837 Vanni Rovighi, Sofia. 'Notes sur l'influence de saint Anselme au XIIe siècle', *Cahiers de civilisation médiévale*, **7** (Oct.–Dec. 1964), 423–37; **8** (Jan.–Mar. 1965), 43–58.

1838 Williams, Schafer. 'Geoffrey of Monmouth and the canon law', *Spec.*, **27** (Apr. 1952), 184–90.

INDEX OF AUTHORS, EDITORS,
AND TRANSLATORS

[Numbers are entry numbers except when otherwise specified]

Abrahams, Israel, 641
Abrahams, Phyllis, 1708
Ackerman, Robert W., 833
Adam de Domersham, *see* Domersham
Adam of Bremen, *see* Bremen
Adam, Robert J., 508
Adams, George B., 248–9, 276, 334, 497
Adams, Norma, 334, 1504
Adkins, W. Ryland, 141
Adler, Michael, 740
Aelred (Ailred) of Rievaulx, *see* Rievaulx
Ailnoth of Canterbury, *see* Canterbury, Ailnoth of
Alexander, Jonathan J. G., 1587
Allcroft, Arthur H., 1195
Allen, Percy S., 642
Anderson, Alan O., 593
Anderson, Mary D., 1625
Anderson, Olof S., 643–5
Anderson, Roger C., 1196
Anderson, Romola, 1196
Andreson, Hugo, 493
Andrew, Walter J., 966, 995
Andrieu-Guitrancourt, Pierre, 1418
Anfray, Marcel, 1626
Anselm, 1706–7
Anstruther, Robert, 1346
Anthony, Edgar W., 1627
ap Ithel, John W., 428
Archer, Thomas A., 336, 1218
Armitage, Ella S., 1197, 1219–20
Armstrong, Aileen M., 646
Arnold, Hugh, 1628
Arnold, Thomas, 447, 458, 461, 1262
Arnulf of Lisieux, *see* Lisieux
Ashley, William J., 955
Aston, Trevor H., 1098–9
Atkin, C. W., 996
Atkinson, John C., 1263–5
Atkinson, Thomas D., 33, 1592, 1629
Attenborough, Frederick L., 208
Ault, Warren O., 277
Aveling, James H., 1419

Baddeley, W. St. Clair, 647, 741
Baildon, W. Percy, 1338
Bain, Joseph, 594
Baker, Alan R. H., 1100–1
Baker, Audrey, 1677

Baker, John N. L., 997
Baker, Timothy, 142
Baldwin, James F., 278, 1198
Ballard, Adolphus, 742–3, 947, 967, 998–9, 1266
Bandel, Betty, 834
Bannister, Arthur T., 34, 648, 1420–1
Barclay, Cyril N., 1199
Baring, Francis H., 539, 1062, 1102–5
Barley, Maurice W., 1082
Barlow, Frank, 143, 331, 337, 429, 540–1, 724, 1345, 1422–3, 1505
Barnes, Patricia, 430, 442, 444, 446, 684, 1274, 1281, 1391
Barraclough, Geoffrey, 338, 430, 649, 835, 872, 931, 997, 1227, 1259, 1532, 1696
Barrow, Geoffrey W. S., 144, 542, 595, 836
Bartholomew Cotton, *see* Cotton
Bates, Edward H., 1267
Bateson, Edward, 145
Bateson, Mary, 146, 339, 948–9, 953
Batsford, Harry, 1593
Baudri de Bourgeuil, 1708
Baudry, Léon, 1787
Baugh, Albert C., 35
Baumgarten, Paul M., 1268
Baxter, James H., 36
Bayart, Jean, 1788
Beeler, John, 1183, 1190, 1221–3
Bell, Alexander, 452, 1789
Bell, Clive, 1630
Bell, Henry E., 1506
Bellot, H. Hale, 1
Bémont, Charles, 209
Benedeit, 1709
Benham, William, 1424
Bennett, Henry S., 725
Bentham, James, 1425
Beresford, Maurice W., 744, 968
Bertrand, Simone, 1678
Besterman, Theodore, 2
Bethell, Denis, 1507
Beveridge, William H., 956
Bickley, Francis B., 661
Bigelow, Melville M., 210, 279
Billson, Charles J., 745
Birch, Walter de Gray, 37, 211–12, 431, 1269
Bishop, Edmund, 1580

Bishop, Terence A., 38, 213, 837, 1106-7
Blair, C. H. Hunter, 340-1
Blair, Claude, 1200
Blake, Ernest O., 432
Blakiston, Noel, 1388
Bliemetzrieder, Franz J., 1780, 1790-1
Bloch, Marc, 147, 726, 838, 1714
Blomefield, Francis, 746
Blumenkranz, Bernard, 1715
Boak, Arthur E. R., 372
Boase, Thomas S. R., 1594, 1679
Bober, Harry, 1138
Böhmer, Heinrich, 280, 1426
Boivin-Champeaux, Louis, 523
Bolgar, Robert R., 1733
Bond, Francis, 1595-7, 1631-3
Bond, Shelagh, 342
Bonser, Wilfrid, 3, 1154
Bony, Jean, 1680-1
Borenius, C. Tancred, 1598
Bosanquet, Geoffrey, 448
Boüard, Michel de, 524
Bouquet, Martin, 433
Bourgeuil, Baudri de, see Baudri
Bourne, Kenneth, 540
Bourrienne, Valetin V. A., 1270
Boussard, Jacques, 343
Boutell, Charles, 39
Boutruche, Robert, 148
Boyce, Gray C., 25
Bradshaw, Henry, 1271
Braun, Hugh, 1201
Bremen, Adam of, 596
Brendon, John A., 40
Brewer, John S., 434, 1272
Bridgeman, Charles G. O., 650, 1273
Bridges, John, 747
Britton, Charles E., 41
Broich, Ulrich, 1770
Brooke, Christopher N. L., 149-50, 498, 543, 1302, 1368, 1496, 1508-11
Brooke, George C., 950, 969
Brooke, Iris, 748
Brooke, Zachary N., 151, 344, 543, 1406, 1511
Brooke-Little, John P., 39
Brown, Carlton F., 1710-11
Brown, R. Allen, 345, 727, 1202, 1274, 1606, 1682
Brown, William, 651, 1275
Brownbill, John, 1265
Brundage, James A., 1224
Bryant, Arthur, 152
Bullock, John H., 1276
Bumpus, Thomas F., 1599
Burne, Richard V. H., 1427
Burton, Frank E., 1000-1

Burton, John, 1277
Bury, John B., p. xi, 375, 630
Butler, Denis, 509
Butler, Harold E., 1368

Cabrol, Fernand, 42
Caenegem, Raoul C. Van, see Van Caenegem
Caley, John, 1298
Calmette, Joseph, 153
Calthrop, Dion C., 749
Cam, Helen M., 5, 154, 281, 346-8, 839-40
Cameron, Kenneth, 652
Campbell, Eila M. J., p. xi, 1002-7, 1015, 1019, 1026-7, 1029
Canivez, Joseph M., 1278
Canterbury, Ailnoth of, 1712
Canterbury, Gervase of, 435
Cantor, Norman, 155, 282, 1512
Capes, William W., 1279
Cappuyns, Maïeul, 1792
Caron, Pierre, 6
Carus-Wilson, Eleanora M., 1008-10
Caspar, Erich, 1280
Cautley, Henry M., 1634-5
Chalandon, Ferdinand, 609
Chamot, Mary, 1636
Champollion-Figeac, Jacques J., 597
Chantor, Hugh the, see Hugh
Chaplais, Pierre, 213, 349, 598, 1281
Charles, Bertie, 653
Chefneux, Helène, 1683
Cheney, Christopher R., 43, 1282, 1428, 1513-15
Chenu, Marie-Dominique, 1750
Chevallier, C. T., 205, 332, 724, 1241
Chevallier, Ulysse, 7-8
Chew, Helena M., 350, 1203, 1225, 1516
Chibnall, Albert C., 750
Chibnall, Marjorie Morgan, 487, 1283-4, 1429, 1517-19
Chrimes, Stanley B., 9, 250-1, 255
Christie, Grace I., 1155, 1637
Christie, Mabel, see Seebohm, Mabel Christie
Christie, Richard C., 436
Christina of Markyate, see Markyate
Christopher, Henry G. T., 44
Church, Charles M., 1430
Church, Richard W., 1490
Churchill, Irene J., 1431
Clagett, Marshall, 585, 1156
Clapham, Alfred W., 1600-2
Clapham, John, 957
Clare, Osbert of, 1713-14
Clark, Andrew, 1285
Clark, Cecily, 437

Clark, E. Kitson, 1286
Clark, George T., 438, 1204
Clark, John W., 1287
Clarke, Adam, 239
Classen, Ernest, 439
Clay, Charles T., 651, 664, 788, 1288, 1520–2
Clowes, W. Laird, 1226
Coggeshall, Ralph de, 440
Cokayne, George E., 45
Colish, Marcia L., 1751
Collar, Hubert, 1289
Colvin, Howard M., 751, 1606, 1684
Constable, Giles, 1432
Cook, George H., 1638–40
Cooke, Alice M., 1523
Copleston, Frederick C., 1734
Corbett, William J., 499–500
Cornford, Margaret E., 654
Cottineau, Lawrence H., 46
Cotton, Bartholomew, 441
Coulborn, Rushton, 841, 936–7
Coulton, George G., 728–9, 1407
Courtney, Francis, 1781
Craig, John H. M., 970
Cramer, Alice C., 351–2
Cranage, David H. S., 1641
Craster, Herbert H. E., 1290
Creighton, Charles, 1157, 1167
Crispin, Gilbert, 1715
Critall, Elizabeth, 1524
Crombie, Alistair C., 1148, 1158, 1168
Cronne, Henry A., 214, 230, 353–4, 525, 544
Crosby, Everett U., 1433
Cross, Frank L., 47
Crossley, F. Herbert, 1603
Crowley, J., 1491
Cunningham, William, 752, 958
Curtius, Ernst R., 1735

Daniel, Walter, 1716
Daniell, F. H. Blackburne, 1685
D'Anisy, Louis Léchaudé, 215
Danks, William, 1489
Darby, H. Clifford, p. xi, 971–2, 996, 1002–7, 1011–16, 1019, 1023, 1025–9, 1032–5, 1037, 1044, 1054–8, 1061, 1083–4, 1108
Darlington, Reginald R., 355, 442, 730, 842–3, 1291, 1492, 1721, 1752
Davenport, Francis G., 1085
David, Charles W., 526, 1793
Davies, J. Conway, 216, 1292
Davies, Maud F., 753
Davis, Godfrey R. C., 48
Davis, Henry W. C., 217, 246, 356, 443, 501, 545–7, 1180, 1525–6, 1572

Davis, Ralph H. C., 214, 444, 527, 548–50, 844–5
Dawson, Charles, 1642
Deanesly, Margaret, 1408, 1794
Delbrück, Hans, 1184
de Ghellinck, Joseph, 1753
Delhaye, Philippe, 1795
Delisle, Léopold, 492
Denholm-Young, Noel, 49, 283, 1293
Dept, Gaston, 610
de Ricci, Seymour, 50
de Roover, Raymond, 1017
Derry, Thomas K., 1149
de Zulueta, Francis, 1732
Dhondt, Jan, 628
Diceto, Ralph de, 445
Dickinson, John C., 1409, 1434, 1686
Dickinson, William C., 611
Dickson, Marie P., 1294
Dietz, Frederick C., 959
Digby, George W., 1169
Dimock, Arthur, 1435
Ditchfield, Peter H., 1604
Dodwell, Barbara, 446, 846–8, 1527
Dodwell, Charles R., 1578, 1643
Dolley, R. H. Michael, 973, 1018
Domersham, Adam de, 1349
Donkin, R. A., 849
Doubleday, H. Arthur, 156
Douglas, David C., 157, 332, 357–9, 494, 528, 551–4, 655–6, 754, 788, 850, 1295–6, 1754–5
Dove, Patrick, 940, 1043
Dowell, Stephen, 284
Drake, Francis, 755
Du Boulay, Francis R. H., 756, 851, 1436
Duby, Georges, 731
Du Cange, Charles, 51
Ducarel, Andrew, 757, 1484
Duckett, George F., 1297
Dugdale, William, 218, 657, 758, 1298, 1437
Duggan, Charles, 1413, 1438
Duncumb, John, 759
Dupont, Étienne, 510
Durham, Lawrence of, 1717
Durham, Symeon of, 447

Eadmer, 448, 1718
Earle, John, 449
Edwards, Edward, 450
Edwards, J. Goronwy, 346, 359–60, 462, 852, 868, 912, 1120, 1540
Edwards, Kathleen, 1439
Ekwall, B. O. Eilert, 52, 658–60, 760–1, 852
Elliott-Binns, Leonard E., 762

75

Ellis, Dorothy M. D., 1528
Ellis, Henry, 1069-70, 1437
Ellis, Henry J., 134, 661
Elmham, Thomas of, 1299
Elton, Charles I., 1086
Emden, Alfred B., 1747, 1796
Evans, Joan, 1644-5
Evans, John G., 1300
Eyton, Robert W., 662, 763-7

Farley, Abraham, 1068
Farmer, Hugh, 1797
Farrer, William, 158, 361, 451, 663-4, 768, 853-5, 1181
Fauroux, Marie, 219
Feilitzen, Olof von, 769
Ffoulkes, Charles J., 1227
Finberg, Herbert P. R., 770-2, 1109, 1440
Finn, R. Welldon, 285-8, 362-5, 972, 1019, 1110-11
Fleming, Lindsay, 1301
Fletcher, Joseph S., 1441
Flete, John, 1442
Fliche, Augustin, 366, 612, 1410-12
Florence of Worcester, see Worcester, Florence of
Floyer, John K., 53
Foliot, Gilbert, 1302
Foreville, Raymonde, 482, 555, 1412
Förster, Max, 1443
Foster, Charles W., 773, 1063, 1303
Fournier, Paul, 1444
Fowke, Frank R., 1579
Fowler, G. Herbert, 54, 665-6, 1087, 1304-5
Fowler, Joseph T., 1306-8
Fox, Levi, 556, 1445
Français, Jean, 11
Fransson, Gustav, 774
Fraser, Henry M., 1064
Freeman, Edward A., 511-12, 557
Frère, Edouard, 12
Frere, Walter H., 1529
Fry, Charles, 1593
Fryde, Edmund B., 118, 1020
Fryde, Michael M., 1020
Furber, Elizabeth Chapin, 20
Furneaux, Rupert, 513
Fussell, George E., 1075

Gaimar, Geffrei, 452
Galbraith, Vivian H., 55-6, 289-90, 346, 367-70, 558, 856, 1530-1, 1798
Gale, Roger, 667
Gamer, Helena A., 1347
Ganshof, François, 133, 159, 608
Gardner, Arthur, 1605, 1659

Garrod, H. William, 642
Gasquet, Francis A., 1580
Gaut, Robert C., 1088
Geffrei Gaimar, see Gaimar
Gelling, Margaret, 668
Geoffrey of Monmouth, see Monmouth
Gervase of Canterbury, see Canterbury, Gervase of
Ghellinck, Joseph de, see de Ghellinck
Gibbins, Henry de B., 960
Gibbs, Marion, 1309
Gibbs, Vicary, 45
Gilbert Crispin, see Crispin
Gilbert Foliot, see Foliot
Giles, John A., 453, 1720, 1731
Gilson, Etienne, 1736-8
Giry, Arthur, 57
Giuseppi, Montague S., 58
Glastonbury, John of, 454
Gleason, Sarell E., 1446
Gloucester, Robert of, 455
Glover, Richard, 1228
Glunz, Hans H., 1447
Gneist, Heinrich Rudolph von, 252
Goebel, Julius, 291
Goodman, Arthur W., 1310
Gorges, Raymond, 775
Gough, John W., 292, 974
Gover, John E. B., 669-76
Grabmann, Martin, 1739
Graham, Rose, 1493, 1532-6, 1799
Gransden, Antonia, 1311
Grant, Francis J., 59
Gras, Ethel C., 776
Gras, Norman S. B., 776
Gray, Arthur, 777
Gray, Howard L., 1076
Grazebrook, George, 677
Green, John R., 502
Greenaway, George W., 157
Gregory VII, Pope, 1280
Gretton, Richard H., 678
Grierson, Philip, 159, 629
Gross, Charles, 13-14, 975
Guilloreau, Léon, 1312, 1537
Guisborough, Walter of, 456

Hadcock, Richard N., 95
Haddan, Arthur W., 1313
Hall, A. Rupert, 1151
Hall, Catherine, 114
Hall, Donald J., 778
Hall, Hubert, 15, 64-5, 224, 951, 976
Hallam, Herbert E., 1089-90
Hallier, Amédée, 1782
Halphen, Louis, 613, 630-1
Hamil, Frederick C., 371-2
Hamilton, Henry, 977

Hamilton, Nicholas E. S. A., 1065, 1350
Hamilton, Sidney G., 53
Hammer, Jacob, 1723
Hammond, Eugene A., 1143
Hanning, Robert W., 1756
Harcourt, L. W. Vernon, 294
Harding, Alan, 253
Hardwick, Charles, 1299
Hardy, Thomas Duffus, 66, 223, 1343
Harland, John, 680
Harmer, Florence E., 225, 439
Hart, Cyril E., 681
Hart, William H., 1314-15
Hartshorne, Charles H., 1205
Hartung, Edward F., 1170
Harvey, Alfred, 1206
Harvey, Barbara F., 1538
Harvey, Henry P., 67
Harvey, John, 1607-8, 1646
Harvey, S., 1021
Harvey, Thomas E., 1783
Haskins, Charles, 978
Haskins, Charles Homer, 226, 295, 373-4, 514, 632, 1159, 1171-3, 1229, 1740, 1757
Haskins, George L., 254, 457
Hassall, William O., 682, 1316
Hatton, Sir Christopher, 686
Haycraft, Howard, 96
Hazeltine, Harold D., 375
Heales, Alfred C., 1317
Hearne, Thomas, 227, 454, 466, 1318-19, 1349
Heaton, Herbert, 961, 979
Hector, Leonard C., 68
Heer, Friedrich, 160, 1741
Hefele, Carl J. von, 1320
Hemmeon, Morley de Wulf, 779
Henderson, William G., 228
Heningham, Eleanor K., 1800
Henry, Desmond P., 1706, 1758
Henry of Huntingdon, see Huntingdon
Herbert, John A., 1581-2
Herbert de Losinga, see Losinga
Hervey, Francis, 683
Hexham, John of, 458
Hexham, Richard of, 459
Hibbert, Arthur, 1022
Hill, Bennett D., 1448
Hill, James W. F., 780, 857
Hilton, Rodney H., 858
Hoare, Richard C., 781
Hodgen, Margaret, 1160, 1174
Hodgett, G. A. J., 859
Hodgkin, Robert H., 503
Hodgson, John, 782
Holdsworth, William S., 255, 296
Holland, Thomas E., 1801

Hollings, Marjory, 1230, 1322
Hollister, C. Warren, 161, 1185, 1207, 1231-8
Holly, D., 1023-5
Holmes, Richard, 1323
Holmes, Urban T., Jr., 1687
Holmyard, E. John, 1151, 1161
Holt, James C., 860, 1238
Holtzmann, Walther, 376, 1324-5
Homans, George C., 861-3
Hope, W. H. St. John, 1342, 1449, 1583
Hoskins, William G., 772, 783-4, 1112-13
Hoste, Anselm, 1719, 1727
Howden, Roger of, 460
Howell, Margaret, 297
Howlett, Richard, 459, 478, 483, 486, 492
Hoyt, Robert S., 16, 298, 377-9, 684, 864
Hudson, William, 952
Hugh the Chantor, 1326
Hughes, Anselm, 1609
Hulton, William A., 1327
Humphreys, Arthur L., 17
Hunt, Richard W., 390, 392, 837, 1334, 1831
Hunt, William, 1328
Hunter, Joseph, 240, 1329
Huntingdon, Henry of, 461
Hurnard, Naomi D., 380-1
Hurry, Jamieson B., 1450
Hutchins, John, 785

Inman, Alfred H., 1066
Ithel, John W. ap, see ap Ithel

Jackson, Thomas G., 1610
Jacob, Ernest F., 346
Jaffé, Philipp, 1330
James, Montague Rhodes, 69-87, 688, 1784
Jamison, Evelyn M., 633
Jaryc, Marc, 6
Jenkins, John G., 666, 1331
Jenkins, Rhys T., 18
Jenkinson, Hilary, 89, 382
Jennings, J. C., 1802
Jensen, Ole, 1539
Jesperson, J. Otto, 88
Jeulin, Paul, 559-60, 634
John, Eric, 732
John of Glastonbury, see Glastonbury
John of Hexham, see Hexham, John of
John of Salisbury, see Salisbury
John of Worcester, see Worcester, John of

Johnson, Charles, 36, 89, 229–30, 240, 383, 462, 866, 1326
Jolliffe, John E. A., 256, 299, 384–5, 867–8
Jones, Arthur, 1540
Jones, Gwilym P., 1175
Jones, Philip, 90
Jones, Thomas, 463–4
Jones, W. H. Rich, 1332–3
Jope, Edward M., 1026
Joüon des Longrais, Frédéric, 300, 869
Jumièges, William of, 465
Jusserand, Jean A., 786

Kantorowicz, Ernst H., 301
Kapsner, Oliver L., 19
Keeton, George W., 302
Kemp, Eric W., 1325
Kendrick, Albert F., 1647
Kendrick, Thomas D., 1611, 1688
Ker, Neil R., 91–4, 1334, 1803
Keyser, Charles E., 1648
Kibre, Pearl, 1139, 1147
Kienast, Walter, 515, 614
Kimball, Elizabeth G., 303
King, Peter, 635
King, S. H., 1027
Kingsford, Charles L., 715
Kinvig, Robert H., 1028
Kissan, Bernard W., 1541
Klauser, Renate, 104
Knowles, David, 95, 1340, 1451–5, 1494, 1542–5, 1804
Koebner, Richard, 870
Körner, Sten, 516
Körting, Gustav, 1759
Kosminsky, Eugeny A., 1091
Koyré, Alexander, 1760
Kranzberg, Melvin, 1150
Krappe, Alexander H., 1176
Kuhn, Sherman, 97
Kunitz, Stanley J., 96
Kurath, Hans, 97
Kuttner, Stephan, 1335, 1546

La Chauvelaye, Jules, 615
Laking, Guy F., 1208
Lambrick, Gabrielle, 1547
LaMonte, John L., 1793
Lancaster, Joan C., 1548
Lancaster, William T., 1336–8
Landgraf, Artur, 1805
Landon, Lionel, 231
Lanfranc, 1339–40, 1720
Lang, Paul Henry, 1612
Langebek, Jacob, 1712
Langlois, Charles V., 600, 1162

Laporte, Jean, 1239
Lappenberg, Johann M., 504, 596
Lapsley, Gaillard, 257, 304, 386, 871, 1240
Larsen, Laurence M., 305
Latham, Lucy C., 872
Latham, Ronald E., 98
Lawrence, C. Hugh, 1413
Lawrence of Durham, see Durham, Lawrence of
Lawrie, Archibald C., 601
Leach, Arthur F., 1341, 1761
Le Bras, Gabriel, 873, 1444, 1549
Leclerq, Henri, 42, 1320
Leclerq, Jean, 1742
Le Couteur, John D., 1649
Lee, Sidney, 127
Lees, Beatrice, 874, 1067
Leff, Gordon, 1743
Legg, J. Wickham, 232, 1342
Legg, L. G. Wickham, 233
Legge, M. Dominica, 1762–3, 1806–8
Lehmann-Brockhaus, Otto, 1584
Leland, John, 466
Lemarignier, Jean F., 1456
Lemmon, Charles H., 1209, 1241
Le Neve, John, 1343
Lennard, Reginald V., 387–8, 733, 875–8, 1114–19
Le Patourel, John, 389–90, 529, 561, 685
Le Prévost, Auguste, 479
Leroy, Alfred, 1613
Lethaby, William R., 1614, 1650–1, 1689
Levison, Wilhelm, 467
Lewis, George R., 980
Lewis, Michael, 1186
Leyser, Karl, 636
Liebermann, Felix, 234–5, 306, 468, 517, 1344, 1809
Liebeschütz, Hans, 1764
Lilley, Alfred L., 1810
Linklater, Eric, 518
Lipson, Ephraim, 962, 981
Lisieux, Arnulf of, 1345
Little, Andrew G., 1526, 1560, 1811
Lloyd, Alan, 519
Lloyd, C. W., 1029
Lloyd, John E., 616
Lobel, Mary D., 787, 1457, 1550
Loewe, Herbert, 641
Longhurst, Margaret H., 1652
Longley, Thomas, 1063
Longuemare, Elie, 333
Loomis, Laura Hibbard, 1653
Loomis, Roger Sherman, 1653, 1690
Lopez, Robert, 163, 1030

Losinga, Herbert de, 1346
Lot, Ferdinand, 1187
Low, Sidney, 100
Loyd, Lewis C., 686, 788
Loyn, Henry R., 164, 391, 734
Luard, Henry R., 441, 469–71, 480
Luchaire, Achille, 602–3
Luders, Anthony, 241
Lunt, William, 1458–9
Lyon, Bryce D., 20, 258, 307, 617, 637, 735, 879, 1242
Lyons, Ponsonby A., 1315
Lyte, Henry C. Maxwell, see Maxwell-Lyte

McCulloch, Florence, 1163
McCusker, John J., Jr., 1031
Macdonald, Allan J., 1495, 1551–2
Mackie, John D., 618
Mackinney, Loren C., 1691
McKisack, May, 392
Maclagen, Eric, 1585
McNeill, John T., 1347
McNultny, Joseph, 1348
Macray, William Dunn, 101, 472–3, 1333
Madan, Falconer, 102
Madden, Frederic, 481
Madox, Thomas, 236, 308, 687
Magoun, Francis P., 1243
Maitland, Frederic W., 259, 265, 393, 735, 880, 953, 982
Major, Kathleen, 1303
Makower, Felix, 1414
Malcolm, Norman, 1812
Malden, Henry E., 165
Mall, Eduard, 1145
Malmesbury, William of, 474–5, 1349–50, 1721
Manitius, Max, 1744
Mann, James, 1210, 1244–5
Mann, James S., 393, 736, 887, 1046, 1167, 1177, 1226
Mann, Max F., 1164
Mansi, Joannes D., 1351
Map, Walter, 688
Marchegay, Paul, 1352
Marcus, Geoffrey J., 1188
Markyate, Christina of, 1722
Marquet de Vasselot, Alphonse J. J., 21
Martin, Charles Trice, 103, 139, 1272
Martin, M. T., 689
Marx, Jean, 465, 562
Mason, John F. A., 394, 563–4
Mason, Robert H., 789
Mason, W. A. Parker, 1553
Massé, Henri J., 1654–5
Matthew, Donald G. A., 166, 1460

Matthew Paris, see Paris
Mawer, Allen, 669–76, 690–5, 1120
Maxwell, Ian S., p. xi, 1014, 1023, 1032–5, 1054–5, 1057
Maxwell, William H., 22
Maxwell-Lyte, Henry C., 1353
Mayr-Harting, Henry, 1354, 1461, 1554
Medley, Dudley J., 736
Meier, Hans, 1138
Mellows, William T., 696
Meredith, Hugh O., 963
Messent, Claude J. W., 1462
Meyer, Otto, 104
Meyer, Paul, 476
Michel, Francisque, 477
Migne, Jacques Paul, 1339
Millar, Eric G., 105, 1586
Miller, E. B., 654
Miller, Edward, 735, 873, 1036, 1463, 1555
Millor, W. J., 1368
Milne, A. Taylor, 1, 23
Misch, Georg, 1765
Mitchell, Jean, 106
Mitchell, Sydney K., 309
Mitteis, Heinrich, 260–1
Molinier, Auguste, 604
Monkhouse, Francis J., 1037
Monmouth, Geoffrey of, 1723
Moore, Grace E., 1724
Moore, J. S., 1121–2
Moore, Margaret A., 24
Moore, Stuart A., 1355
Morant, Philip, 790
Morey, Adrian, 1302, 1496
Morgan, Frederick W., 1123
Morgan, Marjorie, see Chibnall, Marjorie Morgan
Morris, Colin, 395
Morris, William A., 262, 310–12, 396–8, 1246
Mullins, Edward L. C., 107
Munro, Dana C., 25
Murray, Katherine M. E., 313, 1038
Mynors, Roger A. B., 108–9

Napier, Arthur S., 697
Nasmith, James, 1386
Nef, John U., 983, 1039
Neilson, Nellie, 399, 881, 1077, 1092, 1124–5
Nelson, Lynn H., 791
Nevinson, John L., 1692–3
New, Chester, 1464
Newburgh, William of, 478
Nicholas, Frieda J., 951
Nicholl, Donald, 1497
Nicholls, James F., 792

Nichols, John, 793
Nichols, John G., 698
Niermeyer, Jan F., 111
Nineham, Ruth, 400
Noble, William M., 1356
Norgate, Kate, 1247
Noyes, Arthur H., 1189

Oakeshott, Walter, 1656–7
Oakley, Thomas P., 882
Odegaard, Charles E., 401
Offler, Hilary S., 1556
Oleson, Tryggvi J., 314, 402
Oliver, George, 1357, 1465
Oman, Charles, 984, 1190–1, 1211
Omont, Henri, 1557
Onslow, Richard W. A., 530
Oppermann, Charles J. A., 1466
Orderic Vitalis, 479
Ormerod, George, 315
Orwin, Charles S., 1078–9
Orwin, Christabel S., 1079
Osbert of Clare, see Clare

Pacaut, Marcel, 619
Pächt, Otto, 1587–8
Paetow, Louis J., 25
Page, William, 167–96, 803, 985, 1358, 1558
Painter, Sidney, 309, 531, 565, 737, 883–4, 1248–9
Palgrave, Francis, 197, 505
Palmer, William M., 954
Pantin, William A., 390, 808, 1467
Parain, Charles, 1126
Paris, Matthew, 480–1
Parker, Francis H. M., 566
Parker, James, 113, 699
Parker, Thomas W., 1468
Patterson, Robert B., 567
Peck, Heather, 114
Peckham, Walter D., 1359
Pegis, Anton C., 1813
Pellens, Karl, 237
Perkins, Jocelyn, 1360, 1469
Petit-Dutaillis, Charles, 263, 506
Petry, Ray C., 1814
Pevsner, Nikolaus, 1615
Philippe de Thaün, see Thaün
Pike, Luke Owen, 316
Plucknett, Theodore F. T., 264, 270
Plummer, Charles, 449
Pocock, John G. A., 1766
Poitiers, William of, 482
Pollock, Frederick, 265, 885
Poole, Austin Lane, 55, 115, 198, 568, 794, 886, 922, 943, 1009, 1018, 1038, 1112, 1127, 1168, 1244, 1258, 1261, 1545, 1679, 1684, 1692, 1700, 1796

Poole, Reginald Lane, 115–17, 317, 403, 1177, 1180, 1470, 1559–60, 1815–17
Postan, Michael M., p. xi, 838, 873, 1010, 1040–1, 1093, 1128–31
Potter, Kenneth R., 474, 483
Potthast, August, 26
Powell, F. York, 484, 887
Power, Eileen, 986
Powicke, F. Maurice, 118, 520, 1526, 1550, 1560–1, 1716, 1747, 1818
Powicke, Michael, 1192
Powley, Edward B., 795
Prentout, Henri, 532
Prescott, John E., 1361
Prestage, Edgar, 638
Prestwich, John O., 1250–1
Prior, Edward S., 1616, 1658–9
Prothero, Roland E. (Lord Ernle), 1080
Prou, Maurice, 605
Pugh, Ralph B., 199
Pulling, Frederic S., 100
Purser, Carroll, 1150

Raby, Frederick J. E., 1725, 1745–6
Raftis, J. Ambrose, 796, 1471
Raine, James, 485, 1362–3, 1717
Raine, James (the elder), 1472
Rait, Robert S., 620
Ralph de Coggeshall, see Coggeshall
Ralph de Diceto, see Diceto
Ramsay, James H., 507, 987
Ransome, Gwenllian C., 1364
Rashdall, Hastings, 1747
Rathbone, Eleanor, 1546
Rawlinson, Richard, 1473–6
Read, Herbert, 1660
Reaney, Percy H., 119, 700–2
Redford, Arthur, 797, 1042
Reedy, William T., Jr., 404
Rees, William, 18, 120
Reese, Gustave, 1617
Reichel, Oswald J., 888
Reid, Rachel R., 1252
Reidy, John, 97
Renouard, Yves, 639
Rhys, John, 1300
Ricci, Seymour de, see de Ricci
Rice, D. Talbot, 1614, 1618
Rich, Edwin E., 873, 1010
Richard of Hexham, see Hexham, Richard of
Richardson, Henry G., 266, 318, 405–8, 798, 1132, 1819
Richter, Heinz, 1767
Rickard, Peter, 1768
Rickert, Margaret, 1619
Riess, Ludwig, 319, 409

Rievaulx, Aelred (Ailred) of, 486, 1726–8
Rigg, James M., 1498
Riley, James T., 703
Ritchie, R. L. Graeme, 521, 621
Robbins, Rossell Hope, 1711
Robert of Gloucester, *see* Gloucester
Robert of Torigny, *see* Torigny
Robertson, Agnes Jane, 242–3
Robinson, J. Armitage, 799, 1442, 1499, 1562, 1769
Robo, Étienne, 800
Rodgers, William L., 1212
Roger of Howden, *see* Howden
Rogers, Alan, 801
Roots, Ivan Alan, 9
Roover, Raymond de, *see* de Roover
Roper, William O., 1365
Rosenau, Helen, 1694
Ross, Charles D., 1366
Rössler, Oskar, 533
Roth, Cecil, 802
Rothwell, Harry, 456
Round, J. Horace, p. xi, 221, 320–1, 410–13, 522, 534, 569–82, 704, 803–5, 889–908, 1043, 1133–4, 1253–7, 1563
Rousset de Pina, Jean, 1412
Royce, David, 1367
Ruffer, Veronica, 839, 1807
Rule, Martin, 448, 1500
Runciman, Steven, 622
Ruprich-Robert, Victor, 1661
Russell, Josiah C., 806, 909–11
Ruston, Arthur G., 1094
Rye, Walter, 807
Rymer, Thomas, 239

Sabine, Ernest, 1178
St. Joseph, John K. S., 744, 1455
Salisbury, John of, 487, 1368, 1729–31
Salter, Herbert E., 121, 488, 705–6, 808, 912, 1369–71, 1389, 1820–1
Saltman, Avrom, 1501, 1564
Salzman, Louis F., 200, 908, 913–14, 964–5, 988, 1372–3, 1528
Sanders, Ivor John, 122, 1193
Sandys, John E., 1748
Sarton, George, 1140
Saunders, Herbert W., 1374
Saunders, O. Elfrida, 1620, 1662
Saunders, V. A., 1044
Savage, Henry E., 707, 1375
Sawyer, Peter H., 16, 123, 915–16, 1045, 1071, 1319
Saxl, Fritz, 1138, 1663–4
Sayles, George O., 201, 266, 318, 408
Scammell, Geoffrey V., 535
Scammell, Jean, 414
Scherrinsky, Harald, 322

Schirmer, Walter F., 1770
Schlight, John, 1213
Schmitt, Franciscus S., 1707, 1822–3
Scholz, Bernhard W., 1565, 1824
Schramm, Percy E., 323
Schubert, Hans (John) R., 989
Schutt, Marie, 1825
Schuyler, Robert S., 248
Scott, Richenda, 1135
Scott-Giles, Charles W., 39
Sczaniecki, Michel, 1214
Seebohm, Frederic, 917, 1095
Seebohm, Mabel Christie, 1096
Seligman, Erwin R., 124
Setton, Kenneth M., 918
Sharpe, Montagu, 809
Shaw, Stebbing, 810
Sheehan, Michael M., 811, 919
Simpson, Alfred W. B., 267
Simpson, W. Sparrow, 1376
Singer, Charles, 1151
Singer, Dorothea Waley, 1141–2
Sisam, Celia, 1377
Sisam, Kenneth, 1377
Sitwell, George, 812
Slack, Walter J., 920
Slade, Cecil F., 430, 442, 444, 446, 684, 921, 1072, 1274, 1281, 1391
Slicher van Bath, Bernard H., 1081, 1097
Slover, Clark H., 1826
Smail, Raymond C., 1258
Smalley, Beryl, 1771, 1827–9
Smith, Albert H., 708–12
Smith, Arthur L., 1046
Smith, Raymond, 90
Smith, Reginald A. L., 1477, 1566–8
Soehnée, Frédéric, 606
Southern, Richard W., 202, 390, 415–16, 1569–70, 1718, 1772, 1830–3
Spatz, Wilhelm, 1215
Spörl, Johannes, 1773
Spufford, P., 1047
Stapleton, Thomas, 244
Stein, Henri, 28–9, 600
Steinberg, Sigfrid H., 125–6
Steinen, Wolfram von den, 1749
Stenton, Doris M., 203, 268, 686, 813, 922
Stenton, Frank M., 204, 536, 583–4, 669–76, 691–5, 713–14, 814–15, 923–32, 1048, 1169, 1245, 1259, 1378, 1478, 1571, 1678, 1682, 1693, 1704
Stephen, Leslie, 127
Stephens, William R. W., 1415
Stephenson, Carl, 417, 933–4, 990, 1049–51
Stevenson, Joseph, 440, 489, 1379–80

Stevenson, William H., 245, 490, 697, 935, 1073, 1381
Stoll, Robert, 1621
Stolz, Anselm, 1785, 1834
Stone, Lawrence, 1622
Stow, John, 715
Strange, Edward F., 1479
Stratmann, Franz H., 128–9
Stratton, Arthur, 130
Strayer, Joseph, 585, 936–7
Stubbs, William, 246, 269, 435, 445, 460, 475, 1313, 1382–3
Sturler, Jean V., 623, 1052
Suger, 607
Surtees, Robert, 816
Swarzenski, Hanns, 1663
Swynnerton, Charles, 1695
Symeon of Durham, see Durham, Symeon of

Tait, James, 116, 938, 991–2, 1053, 1074, 1260, 1384–5, 1572
Talbot, Charles H., 1143, 1165, 1573, 1722, 1726, 1728
Tanner, Thomas, 1386
Tarleton, Alfred H., 1502
Taswell-Langmead, Thomas P., 270
Tatlock, John S. P., 418, 1774, 1835–6
Taylor, Alfred J., 1261, 1606
Taylor, Charles H., 1793
Taylor, Charles S., 817, 939
Taylor, Frank, 716
Taylor, Isaac, 940
Taylor, John (1829–1893), 792
Taylor, John (1925–   ), 1775
Taylor, Thomas, 1480
Templeman, Geoffrey, 1574
Terrett, Ian B., p. xi, 996, 1012–13, 1025–6, 1028, 1037, 1044, 1054–8, 1061
Thaün, Philippe de, 1144–5, 1164
Thirsk, Joan, 1136
Thomas of Elmham, see Elmham
Thompson, A. Hamilton, 1216, 1416–17, 1481–2, 1665, 1696
Thompson, E. Maunde, 1666
Thompson, James W., 624, 818, 1776–7
Thomson, S. Harrison, 136
Thomson, Samuel K., 131
Thomson, William G., 1667
Thorndike, Lynn, 1146–7, 1152
Thorne, Samuel E., 419, 941, 1575
Thoroton, Robert, 819
Thorpe, Benjamin, 238, 491, 495
Thorpe, John, 1387
Thrupp, Sylvia L., 942
Tierney, Mark A., 820
Tillmann, Helene, 1483

Tindal, William, 821
Tingey, John C., 952
Tipping, Henry A., 1668
Titow, J. Z., 1137
Toll, Johannes M., 625
Tomkeieff, Olive G., 738
Tonnochy, Alec B., 1697
Torigny, Robert of, 492
Tout, Thomas F., 271, 626
Toy, Sidney, 1217
Traill, Henry D., 393, 736, 887, 1046, 1167, 1177, 1226
Treharne, Reginald F., 1778
Tremlett, John D., 1388
Tristram, Ernest W., 1598, 1669
Tselos, Dimitri, 1698–9
Tucker, Susie I., 494
Turberville, Arthur S., 5
Turner, George J., 1389
Turner, Joseph H., 717
Turner, Ralph V., 420
Turner, T. Hudson, 1670
Turner, William H., 718

Ullmann, Walter, 272–4, 421
Unwin, George, 993
Upcott, William, 31
Usher, Abbott Payton, 1153

Vacant, J. M. Alfred, 132
Vacarius, 1732
Valin, Lucien, 324
van Bath, Bernard H. Slicher, see Slicher van Bath
Van Caenegem, Raoul C., 133, 247
Vanni Rovighi, Sofia, 1837
Van Werveke, Hans, 1059
Varenbergh, Émile, 627
Verbruggen, Jan F., 1194
Vercauteren, Lina, 640
Verhulst, Adriaan E., 307
Verlinden, O., 1060
Verrier, Jean, 1590
Vinogradoff, Paul, 739, 822–3
Vitalis, Orderic, see Orderic
von den Steinen, Wolfram, see Steinen
von Feilitzen, Olof, see Feilitzen
von Gneist, Heinrich Rudolph, see Gneist
von Hefele, Carl J., see Hefele
Voss, Lena, 1503

Wace, 493
Wagner, Anthony, 719, 824–6, 943
Walberg, Emmanuel, 1144
Walbran, John K., 1390
Walker, Curtis H., 422
Walker, David, 586–7, 720, 1391

Wallenberg, Johannes K., 721
Walne, P., 1392
Walter Daniel, *see* Daniel
Walter Map, *see* Map
Walter of Guisborough, *see* Guisborough
Waquet, Henri, 607
Warburton, John, 1484
Ward, Paul L., 423
Warner, George F., 134, 1591
Warren, Frederick E., 1393
Waters, Edwin G. R., 1709
Waters, Robert E. C., 537
Watkin, Aelred, 1394
Watkin, Hugh R., 1395
Watt, Donald C., 540
Wattenbach, Gulielmus (Wilhelm), 1330
Weaver, John R. H., 496
Webb, Clement C. J., 1729–30, 1786
Webb, Geoffrey, 1623–4, 1671, 1700
Webb, Philip C., 994
Weinbaum, Martin, 325
Wells, John E., 135
Werveke, Hans Van, *see* Van Werveke
Weske, Dorothy B., 1485
West, Francis, 326
West, James R., 1396
Wheatley, Henry B., 827
Wheatley, P., 1061
Whellan, William, 828
White, Albert B., 275, 327
White, Geoffrey H., 424–5, 538, 588–90
White, Lynn, Jr., 1166, 1179
Whitelock, Dorothy, 205, 494, 722
Whitney, James P., 32, 1486
Wightman, Wilfrid E., 591, 829
Wigmore, John H., 426
Wigram, S. Robert, 1397
Wilkins, David, 1398
Wilkinson, Bertie, 328, 592
Willard, James F., 136

William of Jumièges, *see* Jumièges
William of Malmesbury, *see* Malmesbury
William of Newburgh, *see* Newburgh
William of Poitiers, *see* Poitiers
Williams, D. Trevor, 944
Williams, George H., 329
Williams, Gwyn, 830
Williams, Harry F., 137
Williams, Schafer, 1838
Williams, Trevor I., 1149, 1151
Williamson, Edward W., 1713
Willis, Browne, 1487
Willis-Bund, John W., 206
Wilmart, André, 1779
Wilson, James, 207, 945, 1399
Wilson, Richard M., 946
Winfield, Percy H., 138
Witney, Denis, 1094
Wittkower, Rudolf, 1664
Wood, Margaret, 1672, 1701
Woodbine, George E., 427
Woodcock, Audrey, 1400
Woodforde, Christopher, 1673
Wood-Legh, Kathleen L., 1488, 1576
Woodruff, C. Eveleigh, 1489
Worcester, Florence of, 495
Worcester, John of, 496
Wordsworth, Christopher, 1271
Wormald, Francis, 1401–2, 1674, 1702–5
Wright, Andrew, 139
Wright, Cyril E., 140
Wright, Thomas, 723
Wright, William A., 455
Wrottesley, George, 662, 1403–5

Yeatman, John P., 831
Young, Charles R., 330

Zachrisson, Robert E., 832
Zarnecki, Jerzy (George), 1675–6
Zulueta, Francis de, *see* de Zulueta